Frithy Wood

Restoring the Repertoire

Past, Present, Future

Compiled by

Grenville Clarke

Grosvenor House
Publishing Limited

This book is published by
Grosvenor House Publishing Ltd
Link House
140 The Broadway, Tolworth, Surrey, KT6 7HT.
www.grosvenorhousepublishing.co.uk

A CIP record for this book
is available from the British Library

ISBN 978-1-78623-928-0

THE WILLOW

The Willow is truly an amazing tree
Gutsy, ambitious and brimming with diversity
Offering to cater to all our sustainable needs
Just waiting for us to realise and make good use of its properties
It can be coppiced each year or two quite happily
And gives us a very workable product which is called withe
No other tree is so accommodating
So fast growing, yet also patiently waiting
The perfect alternative to polluting plastic
This tree is truly ecologically elastic
It has the sustainable answers "it's a futures tree"
And as a person who looks forward, it's the tree for me.

Carl Coughlin
Woodland Minds attendee

CONTENTS

ACKNOWLEDGEMENT

Without the help of many people this book would not have been written. Over the years many people have been involved with Frithy Wood and thanks to their contributions we have learned a great deal about its history, wildlife, and the impact it has had on our community.

Three years ago Green Light Trust was fortunate to be able to purchase 21 acres of the woodland with money from the Heritage Lottery Fund, Suffolk County Council, Babergh District Council, the Clark Bradbury Charitable Trust, the Lord Belstead Charitable Trust and the Charles Hayward Foundation. Their support enabled us to restart a traditional coppicing regime in the woodland combined with educational opportunities for a large number of volunteers; hence the title of this book 'Restoring the Repertoire'.

Firstly special thanks should go to the previous owners, the Waspe brothers, who sold us the land. Second to Mr and Mrs Ian and Sue Anderson who own the other half of the woodland, which although it is not open to the public, have generously allowed us to undertake survey work in their part of the wood so that we can develop a more complete picture of the state of the whole wood. Thanks too to our neighbour Peter Strawson who granted us public access over his land so that we can welcome guests into our half of the woodland.

We would also like to thank Jim Brown, Ashley Seaborne, GLT Chair Heather Murphy, and Trustees Tony Booth, Clare Rose and Hugh Wolley. Mark Pritchard brought a fresh mind to the manuscript and helped greatly with scientific detail and continuity. Beverley Fox helped greatly to pull the manuscript together for printing. A big thanks to the many people who had a hand in making the Frithy Wood project happen.

Throughout this book there are various sections where the authors will be acknowledged along with those who have contributed to it in other ways. I hope that by doing so everyone who has helped will have an acknowledgement for their time and effort. If we have missed anyone out I, as compiler, take full responsibility for this and offer my apologies in advance.

Special thanks to Mary Feeney who has acted as an overall editing advisor and has kept us on the straight and narrow throughout the compilation of editorial gathered.

Grenville Clarke *Summer 2016*

FOREWORD

Before Green Light Trust took part ownership of Frithy Wood, it was typical of many of the woodlands found in Suffolk - undermanaged and overrun with deer. Although it had great potential, it also had little social, economic, and biodiversity value.

Frithy Wood lies on an area of clay 'upland'. It sits on an elevated plateau of chalky clay till, laid down by the Anglian glaciation nearly 500,000 years ago. The surrounding area is much dissected by small valleys, giving a markedly undulating landscape with some quite steep slopes. The high chalk content of the glacial till has created a large area of clay soils of the Hanslope series that are good for arable farming.

The purchase of Frithy Wood by the Green Light Trust with funding from the Heritage Lottery Fund and other supporters, has brought this important ancient woodland back to life. It is creating great opportunities for volunteers to work with nature, whilst supporting disadvantaged, vulnerable, and marginalised individuals to develop and move on with their lives. It is very heartening that people are gaining formal careers training as part of this process, and it will be interesting to see where this journey may lead some of those who have participated in the project.

This book was inspired by Professor Oliver Rackham's book, *Hayley Wood: Its History and Ecology*, a book, which for many, first highlighted the importance of ancient woodlands. Although Oliver never quite managed to find the time in his busy schedule to write a book about Frithy Wood, it always held a special place in his heart. He would show his students the historic maps and data held on the wood at the Suffolk Records Office, whilst delivering one of his much celebrated courses on ancient woodland at the Field Studies Council Centre at Flatford Mill. Oliver visited Frithy Wood on many occasions and I know he was delighted that the Green Light Trust were able to buy a large proportion of the woodland, knowing it would be actively managed in a sustainable way, reflecting its historical past.

Frithy Wood is once again a social, economic and environmental asset functioning as it did in the past, using simple tools to cut and harvest coppice. This has been achieved through great partnerships, and working between the Heritage Lottery Fund, the dedicated and skilled Green Light Trust staff, and the many volunteers who have given and gained so much from their work in Frithy Wood. As a result, the purchase, management, and care of Frithy Wood is a great success story.

Gary Battell – Woodland Advisor Suffolk County Council

Oliver Rackham *1939–2015*

INTRODUCTION

From the Palaeolithic times, some 2.5 million years ago, until the present day people have depended on woodlands for food, fuel and as a source of raw materials to make tools, equipment and their homes. This essential connection to woodland has been instrumental in helping the human race to evolve and become, arguably, the most advanced species on our planet.

Around 10,000 BC land became increasingly important for growing crops. Hunter gatherers scattered seed, harvesting and reseeding, and woodlands were cleared to meet the increasing demand for agricultural land to produce food - both crops and livestock. More recently, the growth of consumerism and the pursuit of improved lifestyles has led to substantial changes to our lives. Today, near instantaneous communications, the ability to control our home environments at the flick of a switch and a vast range of convenience foods have changed our lifestyles fundamentally.

The effects are twofold. Firstly, many people no longer view the natural environment as being important, or even relevant to their survival. Many have neither the time nor the inclination to give much thought to the environment. Ironically, their closest connection is often through the purchase of a lottery ticket - the hope of winning millions is helping fund the conservation of our heritage. Secondly, people often now lead a much more sedentary lifestyle. The effects of consuming more calories than needed and a lack of exercise have resulted in an estimated 2 billion people, 30% of the world's population, being obese. The pressures of every aspect of our lives are leading to an increase in mental illness, drug addiction, stress, depression and anxiety at all ages. Green Light Trust brings people and nature together to enhance and enrich their lives and their lifestyles. We do this by reconnecting people with the natural environment through a series of programmes and projects. These encourage people to enjoy being outdoors and protect our environment at the same time. We focus particularly on vulnerable people, for whom being outdoors and learning about conservation can have a profound effect on their wellbeing and approach to life.

'Frithy Wood – Restoring the Repertoire' is a wonderful example of how this works. We hope this book inspires others and leads to an increase in the number of conservation projects managed by the community for the community.

Ashley Seaborne
CEO, Green Light Trust

ABOUT THE AUTHORS

Tom Brown is Green Light Trust's Woodland and Education Manager. Tom joined the Trust in 2013 to manage the Frithy Wood project. Tom has run his own arboricultural contracting company and prior to joining the Trust he was head of the Arboriculture and Forestry Department at Otley College, Ipswich. Tom draws on his passion and enthusiasm for trees and woodlands and his experience and qualifications to inspire the individuals he works with to achieve and contribute to the restoration of Frithy Wood.

Elizabeth Clarke has lived in Lawshall all her life. She has been the Local History Recorder since 1985 and leads the Lawshall Archives Group. Elizabeth worked for GLT for many years leading Rainforest Workshops around the country, and more recently as one of the Community WildSpace leaders. Her interest in Local History began at Teacher Training College and her thesis was about the history of Lawshall and her own farming family.

Grenville Clarke has supported Green Light Trust since its inception in 1989 in a wide variety of roles. From an early age Grenville has been interested in wildlife and spent much of his spare time on the Suffolk coast trapping and ringing birds to help with scientific research into population dynamics of migrant species. After a career in the perfumery sector Grenville retired to spend more time in the woods. Living in Lawshall has enabled him to keep a friendly eye on Frithy Wood. Grenville played a key role in securing the Heritage Lottery Funding for the Frithy Wood Project.

Wendy Cooper has lived in Lawshall for 26 years and for much of this time has been a volunteer with Forest for our Children and Green Light Trust. Wendy has always been interested in nature, and has been birdwatching for over 40 years with her husband, Cliff. Since retiring Wendy has more time to develop her interest in butterflies, keeping a record of the species seen in and around Lawshall.

Nick Sibbett is a professional ecologist who started his career in Suffolk with English Nature, now Natural England. After a period notifying Sites of Special Scientific Interest and leading on Protected Species safeguard, he ended up responsible for managing three

National Nature Reserves and advising on the management of thousands of hectares of SSSIs in Breckland. Following that he became a successful ecology consultant, working with developers and local authorities to ensure that new developments are ecologically neutral or beneficial. In his spare time he is active within Suffolk Bat Group, chairs a thriving Community Woodland group and runs a heathland conservation grazing project.

Angus Wainwright has worked for many years as an archaeologist for the National Trust both in East Anglia and the northern Home Counties. He has a particular interest in woodland archaeology and history and a love of all aspects of the woodland experience – sights, sounds, smells and sensations.

Adrian Walters grew up on a small farm in Suffolk. Following spells of teaching abroad, agricultural contracting work and as a horticultural instructor he took on a countryside management role for a small Suffolk charity in 1990. He is leader of the Silvicultural Group, which manages Golden and Crooked Woods in Lawshall.

RESTORING THE REPERTOIRE

Tom Brown

How it Came to Be

In September 2012 Green Light Trust (GLT) was awarded funding from the Heritage Lottery Fund (HLF) to begin a three year project to purchase part of Frithy Wood and embark on an innovative programme of woodland management. Matched funding was provided through a number of other sources. Although this marked the official start of the project, it was actually the culmination of months of work and years of development, influenced by a long chain of significant events and a long-held ambition, driven in the main by Grenville Clarke.

Since its inception in 1989 GLT has always been a bit different from other environmental charities. Whilst small, it has always punched above its weight with a history its founders can be duly proud of. It all began in 1988, when Ric Edelmann and Nigel Hughes visited the Hunstein Range Forest, deep in the Upper Sepik region of Papua New Guinea. As they explained later in their book *Trees of Paradise*, they learnt that this uniquely rich eco-system consisting of 2,000 square miles of pristine forest was earmarked for the biggest logging operation yet to hit Papua New Guinea. They pledged to support the local people in protecting their unique homeland and the forest is still standing today.

The tribesmen that Ric and Nigel met asked what was happening in the UK to protect woodland and wild spaces for future generations. Realising that more needed to be done at home, they came up with the idea of a body to help UK people, communities and organisations to develop themselves and learn about their relationship with nature. Thus Green Light Trust was established in 1989 as an environmental charity based at Lawshall in Suffolk with the aim of educating and informing the UK public on environmental matters.

In 1993 a small group of people living in Lawshall decided to create their own woodland. They called it 'Forest for Our Children,' and the project started life on a two acre field in Lawshall, part of which was donated by a local farmer. Subsequently more

Kaku Yafei planting Millennium Yew in Golden Wood

Children celebrating tree planting in Golden Wood

land was acquired for tree planting. Today there are two woodlands, covering an area of 22 acres, both managed by the 'Forest for Our Children' WildSpace group. This was the first of over 60 Community-owned WildSpaces created with support from GLT over the next 20 years.

During this period of development GLT moved and reconstructed the Foundry, its award winning carbon-neutral headquarters in Lawshall. Significantly for the future direction of GLT, it became involved with the Forest School programme, particularly the training of staff and promotion of the Forest School ethos within schools. Aided by the Forestry Commission's national support through grants, GLT quickly became and remains a leading and very well respected trainer. The ethos of Forest School reflected GLT's own ethos and this work led the Trust on its first footsteps towards the restoration of Frithy Wood.

Nigel Hughes, co-founder of GLT, recounts the first seeds of inspiration which would eventually become the 'Restoring the Repertoire' project:

> *"When walking in Lawshall's ancient Frithy Wood with Kaku Yafei, chief of the Eagle Clan, Wagu village in the Hunstein Range, Papua New Guinea, I told him that when Ric and I arrived in 1977 and we first walked here I had a distant dream 'to own something like this one day'. This one day was suddenly approaching. Green Light had already established ownership of Crooked Wood and Golden Wood and had successfully initiated Forest for Our Children by, and for, the community. We were planning our succession and I explained to Kaku my vision to include Frithy Wood in Green Light's future.*
>
> *There were two people I needed him to meet: Anthony and Alistair Waspe, the current owners of Frithy Wood who had inherited it from their father. As we walked around the wood Kaku observed and felt the spirit that only an English ancient woodland can have and agreed that it would be a special addition to our existing work."*

GLT continued to develop, and was beginning to engage with those individuals who would go on to form its communities of interest. Initially some pilot work with disaffected young people in a pupil referral unit using a Forest School approach was carried out and reviewed in *Forest School for all* edited by Sara Knight 2011. A three year Eco-minds project, working with people with mental health issues, along with funding to carry out a four year project working with young people Not in Employment, Education or Training (NEET), show that GLT was beginning to take the first steps towards developing an approach that used nature as a means of engaging disadvantaged or marginalised individuals. As part of a conscious decision to support and further this development, GLT created the Greener Lives programme and appointed a director to run it. This moment was pivotal as the director, bringing with him valuable national experience of working with similar cohorts, was now able to drive the work forward. Funding was sought for projects with further groups including disengaged learners in schools and adults in recovery from drug and/or alcohol misuse. These were duly piloted and the evidence used to inform further development, including working with young people with multiple and sometimes profound learning disabilities. At this point in time only two full time employees (including the director) worked within Greener Lives, supported by associate staff where required.

After much work GLT submitted a stage one application to the HLF on August 25th 2011, and four months later was notified that it would receive £35,000 for a five month development phase. This stage broke down into a number of key areas, including: site acquisition; woodland management planning; development of heritage learning modules; design of a woodland interpretation trail; further research into the history of Frithy Wood; and raising of match funding. All of this culminated in the submission of a stage two application to the HLF in June 2012. After waiting for the outcome of the September HLF Eastern region panel meeting, GLT found out that the application had been successful and a total of £485,000 was secured to purchase the section of woodland and deliver the project. In September 2012 an advert for a Woodland and Education Manager was placed and in November 2012 after a rigorous selection process Tom Brown was appointed to begin in January 2013.

The Project

The approved project was ambitious, using an innovative and challenging model to address the main issues facing the woodland, and had the following aims:

- To purchase a section of Frithy Wood for a cost not exceeding £100,000.
- To engage a range of groups in conservation work and skills training within the wood, including 400 people from socially disadvantaged groups, 500 school/college students and 300 volunteers.
- To create trails and provide interpretation of the wood for visitors.
- To recruit a dedicated, full time Woodland & Environmental Education Manager (WEEM).

- To work with partners to ensure that participants in the different programmes have opportunities to continue volunteering after the end of the project in order to sustain the benefits.

Frithy Wood is a Site of Special Scientific Interest (SSSI), and at the beginning of the project was designated by Natural England as being in an unfavourable condition and in decline, although this designation applied to the whole woodland, including the section not purchased by GLT. The condition of the woodland prior to the commencement of the project is best illustrated by the flora and fauna surveys described in the following chapters. However, for the purposes of this chapter, the following summary sets the scene.

The combination of rides closing in and deer pressure had dramatically reduced the abundance and diversity of flora at ground and shrub level in the woodland. Ash dieback (*Chalara fraxinea*) had been identified in the wood at the end of 2012 and tests on trees confirmed its presence. The species composition of the wood was reasonably uniform across the entire woodland, with Ash and Oak the predominant standards, with coppice stools made up of roughly 40% Hazel, 30% Ash and the remainder a mix of Field Maple and Sallow, and with Hawthorn, Silver Birch and Crab apple growing sporadically.

The work of the project to deliver the objectives listed above was facilitated through a range of programmes and courses targeted at GLT's various communities of interest.

Young Futures Course, aimed at young people at risk of not continuing or having left education, training or employment, along with young people aged 16-24 years categorised as not in education, employment or training (NEET). This course was already running as part of another project. It was initially intended to work with Connexions until this organisation was disbanded and then worked with West Suffolk College. Delivered over five days, the course gives participants the opportunity to learn practical woodland skills as well as covering basic theory behind these skills.

Woodland Minds Programme, working with people recovering from mental ill health. Based on a previously successful programme, in this course a group of 4-10 participants attend a seven week programme, for one day per week. It was planned that GLT would recruit a partner organisation to work with, such as Suffolk Mind, in order to recruit participants to the programme. Participants carry out a range of less strenuous woodland management and craft activities.

Woodland Rescue Programme, working with people recovering from drug, alcohol or substance abuse. Having previously carried out pilot work with a group from Open Road, GLT intended to provide partner organisations with the opportunity of bringing groups of 6-10 participants to the woodland to carry out management activities for a single day per week for seven week blocks.

Activities for All, for people with multiple and profound difficulties. This is an extension and broadening of the Activities Unlimited sessions GLT held previously at the Foundry in

Lawshall. Aimed at adults and late teens and intended to be single sessions delivered to groups of 15 participants, it was intended that this course would draw from a greater geographical region than the other groups and would involve special schools and adult provision.

Woodland ACE (Alternative Curriculum Engagement), a programme designed to engage learners who struggle with what the standard curriculum offers. Delivered in the woodland, it allows participants to complete tasks as a group whilst learning about the woodland and the natural processes that occur within it. Predominantly working with students in pupil referral units and those at school who have been removed from all but the compulsory subjects, this course is delivered during five full or 10 half-day sessions as appropriate.

Woodland HEAL (Heritage, Education & Learning), intended to be delivered predominantly by science teachers bringing their students to the woodland, supported by GLT staff. By linking woodland management to the national curriculum we are able to offer students an opportunity to learn about their heritage and to help deliver the curriculum in an inspiring, hands-on way in a wonderful natural environment. This single day course is delivered to entire class groups at Key Stage 4.

Community WildSpace and Woodland Volunteers, single day sessions each focusing on different skills such as woodland archaeology, coppice management, etc. Whilst training days for Community WildSpace Volunteers were promoted to the 58 WildSpace and Woodland volunteer groups which Green Light Trust had helped to establish over the previous 10 years, we wanted to extend these opportunities to other community green space volunteers. We have therefore talked to a range of local groups about our plans to provide skills development opportunities which will improve their heritage skills knowledge for subsequent use at their own sites and sharing with fellow volunteers.

Local Community Volunteers. As an established local charity, we are very much aware of the need to engage with the local community and, in order to support our thinking, Suffolk County Council kindly provided a household socio-economic profiling report that focused on the local area. Frithy Wood is 1.6 miles from both our operational base and Golden Wood (community woodland), and we were confident we could attract community volunteers from neighbouring parishes who are keen to work in ancient woodlands. We also checked population figures for both Lawshall and neighbouring parishes, which together constitute an estimated 4,270 residents. It was planned that these courses would be delivered as half-day sessions, once a month.

CULTURAL AND SOCIAL HISTORY

Elizabeth Clarke

Over the centuries Frithy Wood has been of enormous importance to, and has had a huge impact on, Lawshall village life. This is evident from information in the historical documents available at national and local record offices. There is no doubt that this wood has survived to this day because of the management that took place when the Manor of Lawshall and the villagers were dependent on the products provided by the wood. It is hoped that the recent revival in its management will ensure that the wood survives for many hundreds of years to come.

Unlike any other ancient wood locally, Frithy Wood is uniquely placed in the centre of Lawshall village. The southern ditch and bank alongside The Street were the southern boundary of the wood until the 1950s and meant that, in the past, the wood was accessible to everyone. As you come into the centre of the village today, the Parish Church, Lawshall Hall and Frithy Wood are prominent landmarks.

Frithy Wood, like the church, has been a focal point of the village over the centuries and the presence of both would have been closely linked to the lives of the people who lived in the village. There is no oral evidence of the importance of the wood but there is a wealth of maps and documents which provide an account of the changing ownership of the wood in the past to the present day.

The name Frithy was in use for the wood as early as 1567[1] when it was mentioned in a book of Lawshall Rentals. At this time the wood was estimated at 42 acres;* the document states that the 'great' wood belonged to the Manor of Lawshall and was described in 1567 as of *'great antiquity'*, which could imply that the wood dates back well before the 16th century.

---

* Measurements varied considerably in different periods of history, so we cannot presume that they are equivalent to today's measurements

Amongst woodland experts the current hypothesis of 'ancient woodland' is as follows. If a wood was in existence by 1600, as Frithy Wood was, it was probably a remnant of a medieval working wood that may well have been managed for many hundreds of years. If this is the case for Lawshall we can well imagine the people who lived here working and using this valuable resource for well over a thousand years.

As for most woods, documentary evidence is often not easy to find and references to the actual site will often be 'incorporated and well hidden' in Manorial documents and Court Rolls. The SSSI (Site of Special Scientific Interest) status report from Natural England[2] describes Frithy Wood as 'ancient' and states that there is documentary evidence for the existence of Frithy (formerly Frith) Wood back to 1545. Hopefully someone will find time in the future to take on the exciting challenge of researching this further!

However, there is strong ecological evidence for Frithy Wood being managed over the centuries. The late Oliver Rackham states that the word *Frith* is almost certain to be pre-1066 from Old English *Fyrhp*,[3] and also that an Anglo Saxon word *fyrth*, meaning wood, has given rise to many Frithy Woods.[4] Based on his survey of the hedges in Lawshall researched from data as early as 1642, Rackham states that the village is a typical *'Ancient Countryside Parish'* which means a district that dates predominantly from before 1700; furthermore he claims that about five-sixths of the hedges surviving in the parish in 1986 were older than 1612.[5] A Hedgerow Survey by Clarke & Walters [6] indicates that there may be hedges even older than Rackham claims.

In 1087 Ramsey Abbey was the fourth wealthiest religious house in England, while nearby in Bury St. Edmunds the Abbey of St. Edmund was the fifth wealthiest. At the time of Domesday in 1086 the Abbot of Ramsey owned 8 hides** or caracutes of land in Lawshall which was about 960 acres. The most significant reference in the Domesday survey is note of 30 pigs, which suggests that there was woodland to support 30 pigs, about 40 acres. Ramsey Abbey documents might shed further light on the name of woodland owned by them at the time.

The Manor of Lawshall, and we would like to presume that this included Frithy Wood, was held by the Abbot of Ramsey from 972 until 4th March 1539/40, when the Abbey was dissolved and was 'granted' to Richard Williams (d. 1544),[7] who was the nephew of the wife of Thomas Cromwell. However, it is suggested [8] that the Abbot of Ramsey continued to be Patron of All Saints' Church until 1546, when Copinger [9] in 'The Manors of Suffolk' states that the Manor was granted to John Rither. Oliver Rackham visited Frithy Wood in 1982 and in the history section of his report wrote as follows. *"At the break up of Ramsey Abbey estates, Lawshall, with its wood of 41 acres, was granted in 1545 to Prince Edward's Cofferer"* (who was the principal officer in the court).[A] There is also a lease of 1547 which specifies

** One hide was c. 120 acres of land

"'all that wood and waste' (boscum et vastum) called Lawsell Woode containing by estimate forty-one acres".[B] By 1547 we believe the Manor of Lawshall was sold to Sir William Drury. Lawshall Hall was probably built or remodelled soon after this, as it is recorded that the date over the door of the Hall was 1557.

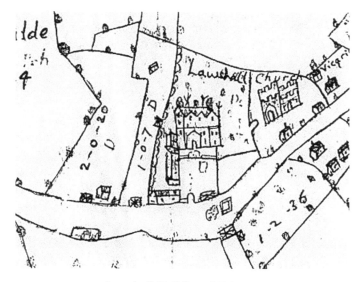

Lawshall Hall from 1611 map

Oliver Rackham also refers to a detailed wood-lease,[C] dated 1621, of *"the ffrith alias the great wood and other groves. All the underwood is to be felled for the best benefitt of the Slopp and Springe"* (i.e. the poles and regrowth). The name *Ffrith* is of note; does this refer to the site of 'our' current Frithy Wood? The names Ffrith and Lawshall Woods are mentioned in documents, but it cannot be presumed that these woods definitely refer to the current Frithy Wood.

What will always be of importance, however, is evidence that shows what impact Frithy Wood, or any other wood, had on the village and how, until very recent times, the products from the wood were vital to the life of the parishioners. Evidence from a survey[10] stating occupations from 1550 to 1912 strongly indicates how the wood may have been utilised. Of course, a prime use of timber would be for house building and we have some houses in the village dating from the 16th century which would, most probably, have used wood from the nearest source. Among the trades of interest mentioned are wheelwright, collarmaker, sawyer, carpenter, cordwainer (who would use wooden lasts), cooper, timber master, rake maker and hurdle maker. It is likely that the wood needed for these trades came from Frithy Wood.

From the 1600s onwards Lawshall has a collection of maps and aerial photographs which relate directly to Frithy Wood. The earliest map of 1611[11] shows 'Frithe Woode', 55 acres

Frithy Wood 1611 Map

2 roods 8 perches ***, belonging to Sir Henry Lee, and along four of the wood boundaries the years of coppice growth are noted. The map is superbly detailed and shows hundreds of tiny fields and innumerable hedgerows and field trees. Coppicing is shown by *"2 years Groth, 10 years Groth and 12 years Groth"*, written in different parts of the wood; looking at the map really feels like stepping back in time.

It appears that the wood was demesne land, which was land retained by the Lord of the Manor for his own use under his management. Ten years later a document [12] from 1ˢᵗ February 1622 states that Sir Robert Lee agreed to sell to Giles Clarke of Lawshall, yeoman, and Robert Clarke of Lawshall, yeoman, *"all underwood and bushes in woods and groves of Manor of Lawshall called the Frith alias the Great Wood, and Kinges Wood, Apledayewood and Upfeild Grove in Lawshall, except timber trees, beech trees, pollards and trees left for stands"*. Along with the 1611 map this is the first direct reference to the wood being managed.

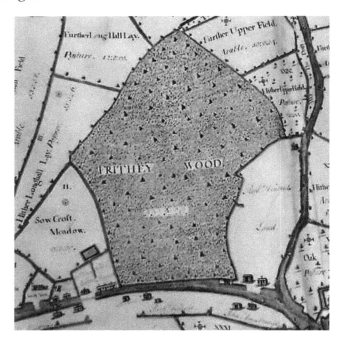

1752 map of Frithy Wood

*** One acre = 4 roods and one rood = 40 perches

12

The second oldest map known is from 1752[13] and shows *Frithey* Wood as part of the survey of the Estate of Lawshall. The wood is included as land belonging to Hall Farm in the occupation of John Smith and the acreage is 53 acres, 3 roods, 2 perches; the wood also appears to be included in a column on the table that includes it as *'profitable'*.

In 1842 the village was surveyed and the Tithe Map produced and this was followed by OS Maps and aerial photographs all of which show, up until 1959, Frithy Wood in its entirety with a boundary identical to that in 1611. In September 1917 details[14] are available of the sale of Lawshall Hall Estate, including Frithy Wood, *"to be worth £60 per annum"*. It was sold by Lord Saumarez, who was Lord of the Manor, and purchased by the then occupier Mr. Herbert Harvey for £900. Hopefully more details about Frithy Wood will be revealed in the estate papers[15] for Lord Saumarez who, until the last century, held the Lordship of Lawshall Manor.

Lawshall Hall 2008

The most recent document[16] is dated 1957, when the then owner of Frithy Wood, Mr. W.G. Waspe, applied for a felling licence to clearfell four acres of oak and ash trees in the wood. In September 1957 a timber merchant offered a quote to fell the trees, including two elms and twenty standing trees. This may be the first time, since the earliest records, that the boundary of Frithy Wood changed. Mr. W.G. Waspe, in a letter to the Conservator of the Forestry Commission, when asking for permission to fell trees, states that he needs *"a great quantity of stakes, rails, posts etc for fencing round my flocks of sheep and other stock"*; he also says that *"at present we are very short of labour on our farms, but if the position should alter we might be able to improve the woodland and in the meantime I will see that anything which looks like growing into a tree is left when we are cutting poles"*. This letter clearly shows the intention of this farmer to maintain and manage Frithy Wood and also how vital the wood was to his livelihood.

Signs of more recent use of the wood included two Anderson shelters for the pigs which were kept in the wood in the 1970s and as a result some trees show signs of scoring by the pigs.

The Waspe family continued to coppice compartments of the woodland up until 2005. Currently Green Light Trust manages 21 acres of the woodland with the help of a wide range of groups who come to discover and enjoy the pleasures of woodland activities. Frithy Wood is still an integral part of village life and is enjoying a renaissance following the new management regime started in 2012 by Green Light Trust. Lawshall village and parishioners should be rightly proud to have this amazing resource on their doorstep.

Acknowledgement

Photograph supplied by Elizabeth Clarke.

SILVICULTURAL HISTORY

Grenville Clarke and Wendy Cooper

Woodland history in the south of England starts around 8000 BC; before this vegetation existed but various glacial periods wiped it away. With the retreat of the last Ice Age our most recent woodlands started to evolve.

The earliest woodland was formed by pioneer species of trees such as Birch *(Betula pendula)*, followed by other species such as Scots Pine *(Pinus sylvestris)*, Pedunculate Oak *(Quercus robur)*, Elm *(Ulmus sp.)* and Hazel *(Corylus avellana)*. This early post Ice Age tree mixture can still be seen in much of Scotland today; as yet the more southerly species, including Beech *(Fagus sylvatica)*, Hornbeam *(Carpinus betulus)* and Cherry *(Prunus avium)*, are not abundant there. Frithy Wood is fairly typical of southern lowland semi-natural woodland found on heavy clay soils.

Human influence on forests was initially small; hunter gatherers were using the woodlands but settlements had not yet started to make an impact. Natural events did have an influence; for example, we know from pollen samples from ancient ponds and bogs that one of the largest events was the severe decline of elm from about 3100 to 2900 BC.

In Suffolk, it was on the lighter soils of the Brecks and coastal areas where destruction of woodland took place. Grazing by domestic animals would have contributed to this deforestation, as well as felling and fire. It is thought that the landscape we see today is very much like it was in about 1200 AD.

This brings us to Frithy Wood, which was probably not cleared, like others in this part of the county, partly because it was situated on high wet heavy land which the plough could not break, and partly because during the Middle Ages woodland had a greater value than arable land. The Lord of Lawshall retained direct ownership of the wood, whereas much of the rest of the estate was rented out.

Frithy Wood is a very good example of an ancient Suffolk woodland situated on wet heavy clay with interesting plant and wildlife communities.

Oliver Rackham visited the wood in 1982[1]. His notes from that visit offer an interesting snapshot:

Vegetation

Surviving wood is a well-preserved coppice. Timber trees Oak, some Lineage Elm variable in numbers, often very large and spreading. Coppicing ceased about 1949 but was revived with the felling of 2½ acres in 1980.

Most of wood is a complex mosaic of Mixed Hazel, Ash-Hazel, and Maple-Hazel; these are associated with aspen clones (thickly scattered, especially in Mixed Hazel), Wych-Elm (single stools, probably more abundant than in any other Suffolk ancient wood), and Cherry (marginal). There are six pockets of Lineage Elm, the largest of some 3 acres and mixed with hazel and other trees. Two small Elm Invasions. Big coppice stools: Lineage Elm (6 ft), Maple (5 ft), Ash (4 ft). **Note - Rackham measured the diameter of stools, we today tend to measure the girth.** *Frequent pole-sized oaks and some young sallows. Elm Disease is severe, with most of the Wych-Elm dead; Lineage Elm killed to base; Ulmus minor less affected.*

Ground vegetation dominated by brambles (Rubus fruticosus aggregate, some Corylifolii). Extensive patches of dog's-mercury especially in S and NE of remaining wood. No large waterlogged areas; oxlips widely but thinly scattered. Patches of nettle in E of wood.

Growth of coppice panel quite good despite deer. Hazel is usually bitten once but then grows away. Coppicing plants rather few (meadowsweet, willowherbs); ground is soon overrun with brambles.

Since Rackham's visit the wood has changed in character with the loss of nearly all the elms to Dutch Elm Disease (*Ophiostoma ulmi* and *O. novo-ulmi*), the increase in deer grazing, and now the onset of Ash dieback (*Chalara fraxinea*). Throughout much of the wood the understorey is rather weak due to over standing (shading) by timber trees (ash and oak), as well as unchecked grazing by deer, rabbits and hares. As a result of the management regime recently introduced, the newly protected coppiced areas are looking good, and layering of hazels has taken place. Planting of new standards will need to be undertaken at some point in the future, in order to replace dead and dying trees.

Although the wood does not contain a large number of tree and shrub species, it still has a magical feel to it with a lovely rich mixture of trees in all stages of development, from the newly coppiced compartments to the old standards and neglected areas. Together they produce an array of habitats providing colour, light and shade, which attract a constantly changing population of plants, insects, birds and animals.

Some of the more important trees found in the wood are described here.

Mature Oak with wood pasture beyond

Oak *(Quercus robur)*

Oaks are the most important and valuable source of timber in the wood. It has been suggested that England was 'built on oaks', showing its huge importance to the nation. With its strength, durability and attractive grain oak was put to many uses. The most well-known use was for ship building, which continued until the 19th century. The Royal Navy was always keen to ensure that there was enough material to meet its needs and encouraged woodland owners to grow oak wherever possible.

Locally, many houses and farm buildings, including Lawshall Hall, were constructed using oak from Frithy Wood. Furniture, posts, gates, carts and tools all used oak. Coopers Farm in the village was probably named after the trade of barrel making which was practised there and would, of course, have used local oak.

Pigs were grazed in the wood when the acorns started to fall, and the bark of oaks was stripped off

Mature Ride Side Oak

in order to make tannin to cure leather. If this is not enough to illustrate the value of the oak tree, consider that there are about 750 mites, insects and lichens which live on oaks, making it the most biodiverse tree in England.

Today there are about 160 standard trees in the wood (there are no coppiced oaks), and the majority have a girth of 2.0 to 2.5 metres, which would suggest that they are all about 150 to 200 years old. There are a few specimen trees with girths measuring more than 3.5 metres, which are estimated to be at least 300 years old.[2] There are only a handful of young oaks throughout the wood, which suggests that woodland management lapsed in the early 20th century, and new trees were not planted to provide the future crop of timber 200 years hence. Today it is imperative to start planting new oaks, in order to ensure the continuity of healthy oaks in the wood for the future.

Ash damaged by pigs

Ash *(Fraxinus excelsior)*
Ash dieback *(Chalara fraxinea)* is now well established in East Anglia and was found in Frithy Wood when the disease was first seen in England in 2012. A number of the larger trees are affected but it is most visible in new growth where coppicing has taken place. Ash is by far the most common large tree in Frithy Wood and its demise will have a great influence on the future structure and management of the woodland. Many of the ash stools were last coppiced in the 1970s; when these are removed they will leave a large gap in the wood which will be filled either by natural regeneration or by the planting of alternative species.

Stored Ash Stool

There is evidence of an interesting forestry practice which took place in the '40s and 50s. In 20 ash stools a single stem was left to grow on into a timber size tree, while the other smaller shoots coming from the base continued to be cut on a regular coppice rotation. These stored stools could be a form of insurance policy whereby, if the value of timber dropped, the stool could be reverted to the conventional form for the production of ash poles.

It is sad to think that future generations will not see the numbers of ash trees we are used to. We will be losing one of our best sources of firewood, a tough, flexible timber for furniture, tool handles and hay rakes (there was a rake factory in the village), and material for fencing. Forty years ago the author owned a Morris Traveller with a lovely exterior ash frame, which survived a rear end crash with a bus in Maidenhead; the car drove off and the bus was towed away.

Hazel *(Corylus avellana)*

This is the most common tree/shrub in the woodland and provides the underwood cover for Frithy; we estimate that between 50% and 60% of the woodland cover is provided by hazel. Many stools are quite old, 200 to 300 years; they are over stood (shaded out) by standard trees, and have been attacked by deer, hares and rabbits. Some have died, therefore layering for two year old coppice hazel will help to produce new plants in the fenced off compartment that has recently been established. In the western part of the wood, the quality and more regular distribution of stools suggest that this area was more intensely managed than the rest.

Hazel is a very versatile wood providing materials for a range of products, including the production of wattle for infilling between beams using daub and wattle, and fencing hurdles. Locally, with a prize flock of Suffolk sheep based at Lawshall Hall, hurdles were being made using hazel from Frithy into the 1960s. Local thatchers were also cutting hazel to use as spars and pegs to hold the thatch in place.

We must not forget the hazel nut which contributed to the diet of our ancestors and still does today for deer, mice and squirrels.

Weak Hazel suffering from shade cover of standard trees.

Coppiced Field Maple

19

Field Maple *(Acer campestre)*

About 3% of the woodland is covered by field maple, all of which has been coppiced. Some are old, with an estimated age of about 300 years. Field maple is a lovely compact tree which provides colours in the autumn as well as good quality firewood. It has been sought after for its rippled veneer for furniture but, in our case, it has been relegated to firewood status. It could well be that with the gaps left by dead ash trees, field maple could start to colonise these clear areas.

Cherry *(Prunus avium)*

There is a single specimen of cherry which is about 50 years old and in good health. It is not visible from our part of the wood.

Crab Apple *(Malus sylvestris)*

There are a few sizeable crab apples in the south and eastern compartments of the wood. Although it is difficult to age this species, we would guess that ours are about 75 years old. The woodsman would have left these trees for their fruit, which is ideal for jams and jellies, as well as providing a good food source for wildlife.

Wych Elm *(Ulmus glabra)*

Two specimen trees of wych elm can be found near the pond in the centre of the wood, as noted by Rackham in his 1982 survey. The trees appear to be in good health; we estimate them to be about 200 years old.

Mature Crab Apple

Wych Elm

Hornbeam *(Carpinus betulus)*

There is a single mature coppice stool of hornbeam which we have highlighted on the route of the recently established circular walk in the wood. Trees are difficult to age but we believe that this tree could possibly be up to 450 years old, the most ancient tree in our wood[3]. After some searching, we found a small number of seedlings which have been transplanted into the Green Light Trust tree nursery to develop safely. It appears that all newly emergent seedlings have in the past either been grazed off or shaded out. It is planned to clear round the parent tree and reintroduce the saplings to produce a hornbeam glade for future generations.

This is one of the most impressive trees we have in the woodland and it is worth dwelling on its long life. It is interesting to think that this

Old coppiced Hornbeam

tree emerged during the reign of Henry VIII. It was 40 years old when the Gunpowder Plot took place, then, just after its 100th birthday, the Great Fire of London occurred. In the next two centuries the Treaty of Union was agreed between Scotland and England, income

Close up of Hornbeam stool

21

tax was introduced and women were allowed to enter Oxford and Cambridge Universities. It survived two World Wars and, finally, in 2015 suffered the indignity of having its girth measured to determine its age.

We should also mention charcoal, which was produced from all of the trees above and was an important product for blacksmiths, furnaces and in the production of gunpowder

Over its life Frithy Wood has provided materials to help warm, feed, house, shelter and provide employment for our community. Now, through the HLF grant, it is providing employment, education and the opportunity to improve the health and wellbeing of those who use the wood.

Through the coppicing regime the health of the wood is improving, but there are threats to our wood because of an increasing number of diseases attacking trees throughout Europe, affecting oak, spruce, alder, plane and horse chestnut. We have just a few species within our wood and in the future one can expect to see new species introduced to help increase resilience to these threats. However woodlands have a degree of in built resilience: can you spot where a large area of elms were growing in the wood in the 70s and 80s before Dutch elm disease killed them?

Frithy wood will continue to be a major social and environmental asset to our village.

Acknowledgement

Photographs supplied by Ruth Clarke and Elizabeth Clarke.

ARCHAEOLOGY AND LANDSCAPE SURVEY

Angus Wainwright

These observations were made by Angus Wainwright following survey work carried out by local volunteers. Earthworks were interpreted using sources supplied by Elizabeth Clarke. Main sources included a 1611 survey by Ralph Treswell; a map of 1752; OS 1:2500 (1884 map); modern OS map; and low resolution Environment Agency LIDAR (Light Detection and Ranging) data mapping.

Introduction

Oliver Rackham visited Frithy Wood in 1982 and produced a detailed report on the wood summarising the history, describing the ecology and also sketching some of the earth-works. This report should be seen as an addition to this.[1] It makes a more detailed survey of the archaeology and suggests some phases of the wood's history not so far revealed by documentary research.

Earthworks were surveyed during the winters of 2014/15 and 2015/16. The first survey was carried out using a compass and 30 metre tape whilst in the second survey earthworks were sketched. These need to be resurveyed in the future at the same accuracy as with the first survey.

Summary

The northern end of the wood is characterised by the presence of a large number of banks creating small irregular compartments. It seems probable that these were originally fields which were absorbed into the wood before it was surveyed in 1611.

Earthworks are represented by a number of banks and ditches, an area of quarrying including a pond, and an artificial fox earth.

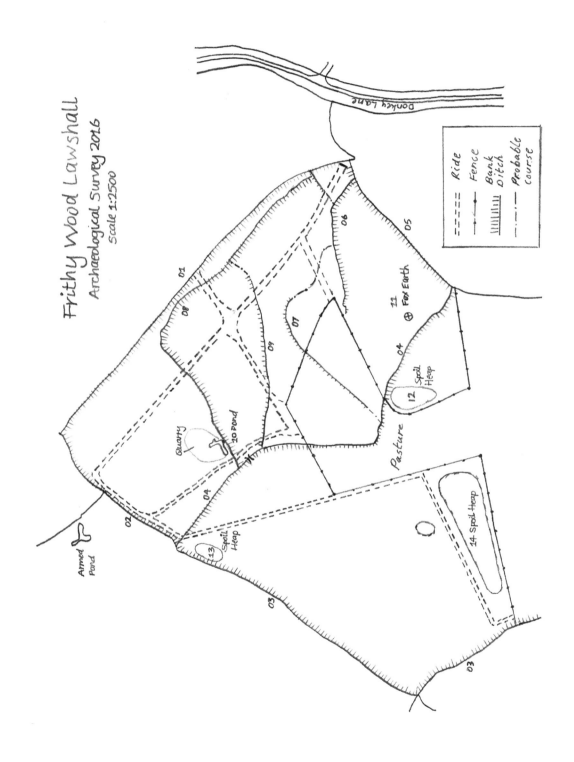

Frithy Wood Lawshall
Archaeological Survey 2016
Scale 1:2500

Ride
Fence
Bank
Ditch
Probable
course

Donkey Lane

01
08
09
07
06
05
11 Fox Earth
04
12 Spoil Heap
Pasture
Quarry
10 Pond
04
02
Armed Pond
13 Spoil Heap
03
14 Spoil Heap
03

Description of Features

The numbers refer to the features on the sketch map.

01 northeast wood boundary. A relatively small bank with a deep functioning ditch outside the wood. Bank width up to 2 metres, ditch width up to 3 metres. Bank relatively sharp profiled.

02 continuation of 01 on northwest boundary to junction with 03. Very weak or absent bank with deep functioning ditch. A weak scarp may be present parallel to the bank inside the wood.

03 continuation of the northwest boundary from junction with 02. At the junction is a distinct kink in the wood boundary. A large eroded bank with a functioning ditch. Bank width up to 4 metres wide and 70 centimetres high, ditch 3.5 metres wide.

Above: Bank and ditch ref 03 northwest section
Below: Northern Section Ref 04

04 large eroded bank and shallow ditch running from junction of 02 and 03 to the southeast woodland boundary – 05. Ditch on the north side. Bank width up to 3.5 metres, ditch width up to 2 metres. This feature has been partially ploughed out where it crosses the field but is traceable as a slight hollow. Rackham shows the section in the field more clearly, so ploughing since his visit may have further damaged it. His survey shows a distinct kink in the section of the field.

05 southwest boundary of wood. Bank with functioning ditch outside the wood. Bank width 3 metres, ditch width 3.5 metres.

06 bank and ditch running from close to the entrance gate to the field. Ditch on north side. Bank width 2.5 metres, shallow ditch width 3 metres. The feature is ploughed out at its west end. Possibly may have turned

sharply to continue as 07 or possibly to the southwest parallel to the field fence to join 04.

07 short section of bank and ditch at the east end of the field. The feature is clearest outside the field but continuing within the field as a shallow hollow running to the south of two oak trees. Ditch on north side. Bank width 2.5 metres, shallow ditch width 2 metres. This feature was difficult to follow in a currently (2016) active area of coppicing but may turn sharply to form a continuation of 06 or the feature may continue to join 06 about half way along its length. This feature needs further examination.

08 a large bank and ditch running northeast from 04 before turning southeast running parallel to 01. Bank width 3 metres, ditch width 3.5 on north side of bank. Bank about 30 centimetres high. The east terminal of the feature close to the woodland entrance is unclear: a short section of bank running at right angles to 08 (southwestwards) may be the same feature originally joining 06 or a later feature. Rackham shows this feature continuing to join 05; if this is correct, the short right-angle bank may be of very recent origin.

09 a much eroded bank and ditch running east from 04 to join 08. Bank width 3.5 metres, ditch width 2.5 metres on south side. The feature is difficult to follow where it is perhaps damaged by the pig farming.

10 a shallow area of quarrying. An irregular area about 20 metres by 20 metres. Runs up to bank 08 but does not cut it. There is an L shaped pond at its south edge up against the bank. The pond is sharp profiled and probably a later adaptation of the quarry. The pond is shown on the Old OS map.

11 An artificial fox earth close to the east end of 04. Composed of a squarish mound over a part collapsed brick chamber. Two arms extend from the chamber for about 7 metres made of large yellow ceramic drainage pipes (c. 10 inch) partly covered in soil.

12, 13, 14 large irregular soil heaps containing a few oak stumps. Probably heaps from the clearance of coppice stools which, apart from the few oak stumps, have now rotted away. 13 is in a surprising position some distance from obvious clearance areas.

15 roughly circular depression – possibly a now dry pond.

Drainage grips. Shallow and narrow ditches with no discernible bank which tend to take a wandering path into a nearby ditch. Used to drain the woodland. These features are common in the wood but were not surveyed. It would be interesting to at least plot their distribution as they may show different management by owners or areas where surface features have been bulldozed.

Interpretation

It is possible to suggest a model for the development of the wood. Bank 04 may represent the original northern end of the wood. The area enclosed by 08 seems to have been added into the wood at a later date. This additional area is divided into three compartments; these could be wood compartments suggesting a smaller wood absorbed into the bigger one or, more likely, three small fields. These fields would be similar in area to the small fields to the southeast, shown on the 1611 map and tenanted by William Cawston. Subsequently, but before 1611, another area has been added by the construction of boundaries 01 and 02; this squared off the northwest corner of the wood and added a long strip at the north end. A possible reason for adding this strip was to provide an access track within the wood. If this new area was taken out of fields one would expect to find some remains of boundaries crossing this narrow strip – these were not found. The unusual curving rather than right-angled corner of 08 is also an interesting feature. Taken together they might suggest that the wood was carved out of a common to the north, which was later enclosed and formed Upfolde Field on the 1611 map. Rackham suggests this enclosure may have been the result of formalising the encroachment of the wood into the adjoining field. The small size of the boundaries 01 and 02 suggests a date of construction not long before 1611, whilst the larger boundaries within the area enclosed by 08 suggest a medieval date whatever their function. Rackham notes that the wood was estimated as 41 acres in 1545 but by 1611 it was 55 acres; it therefore seems likely that this enclosure happened between these dates. Feature 08 and feature 02, which must be contemporary with it, are on the same scale as the original medieval boundary 03.

The quarry and pond (feature 10) appear to derive from superficial working of surface clay, probably for brick making, possibly before its enclosure into the wood but just as likely afterwards. The clay may have been taken to another kiln site but evidence for burnt clay and brick fragments should be sought in the vicinity of the feature. The pond is quite sharply profiled indicating a more recent origin, possibly as a flight pond to attract ducks for shooting. Feature 15 is a more ancient feature, possibly a dried and silted pond.

The artificial fox earth (feature 11) may possibly be dated from the bricks and pipes used. Such structures were constructed from the Victorian period to recent years in fox hunting country. They could be used in a number of ways to try to guarantee a fox would be found in the most advantageous position for the hunt.

Some observations on the map evidence

1611 map. This map appears to be an accurate survey and would probably repay digitisation and overlaying on modern mapping. In the region of the wood there are several points of interest. The cottage by the lane is shown with a plot stretching towards the wood and explaining a right-angle bend in the wood boundary on later maps. The site of the cottage can still be located beside the lane. On the other side of the wood the unusual armed pond can be seen (a type of pond noted by Rackham but difficult to explain). No features are shown within the wood but of most interest are the annotations along the boundary indicating 2, 3, 10, 12 years' growth. This presumably refers to the age of the coppice and suggests that the wood was then divided into 4 compartments; unfortunately the compartment boundaries are not marked. Other woods are annotated similarly. The lease quoted

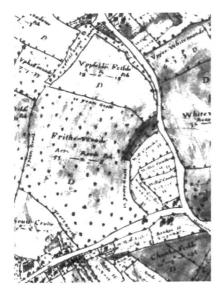

1611 map of Frithy Wood

by Rackham in 1621 has the wood then divided into five 10 acre compartments.

1752 map. This is less useful: the landscape seems stable but, if the detail is to be believed, there is less wood pasture.

1884 OS map. This is an extremely detailed map revealing much interior detail of the wood. Individual hedgerow trees are surveyed accurately and marked as normal with a tree with a small shadow to the right and a small backward 'c' shape inside. By this time there is little wood pasture in the area of the repro-duced map, perhaps indicating a conversion of pasture to arable. The cottage remains but the plot behind has been removed. Within the wood itself the most obvious features are the woodland drives, which emanate from four entrance points, the most obvious being at the south in the village. These drives are rather meandering; however, the wood is also quartered by straight drives which do not emanate from the entrances. One could guess that the meandering drives are the original routes and the straight ones later additions, perhaps to aid game bird shooting. Unless it is an ink spot, there appears to be a small building at the centre of the wood, either a woodman's or gamekeeper's hut. The pond is also clearly marked. Most unusually it appears that the surveyor has chosen to survey the standard trees within the wood. Normally only a woodland symbol is used which does not differentiate between coppice and coppice with standards, nor in any way suggest the density of standards. If the surveyed tree symbols are an accurate representation it would indicate a density of standards at 5 per acre. It is noticeable that there are few standard trees actually on the wood bank but there is a distinct line of trees just within the wood parallel with banks 01 and 02. Some of the larger oaks in the wood can be found beside bank 01 and these may be some of the ones shown on the map. A few oak stumps can be found in the non-bulldozed areas: these may well be some of the trees shown and felled within the last hundred years (oak stumps are surpris-ingly long lasting). This could be confirmed by further survey in the future. The stumps of other species may have rotted away. No pine trees are shown.

LIDAR. LIDAR is an airborne mapping technique which uses a laser to measure the dis-tance between the aircraft and the ground, allowing highly detailed terrain models to be generated. The Environment Agency uses LIDAR to map the English landscape and the resulting data are publicly available for use in archaeological and other surveys. Although low resolution, the LIDAR map for Frithy Wood shows up most of the surveyed features, albeit weakly.

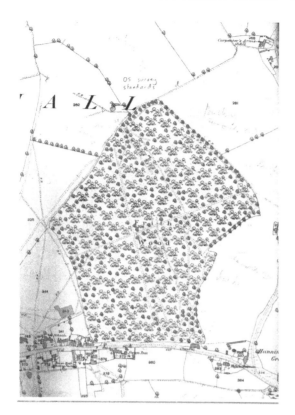

1884 map, standards highlighted
O.S

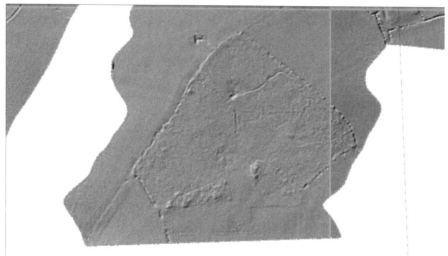

Frithy Wood 2m resolution LIDAR

Acknowledgement

Survey team – Andy Limmer, Wendy Cooper and Grenville Clarke, and Survey Map by Andy Limmer.

FLORA

Adrian Walters

A walk in any ancient woodland takes one away from the pressures of the modern world. As soon as one enters the woodland the weight of 21st century life begins to drop away and the deeper into the wood one walks the more the cares of the world seem to be left behind. It would appear that ancient woodland might be rather good for our health. Of course, almost everyone appreciates trees and it may be as simple as that. Ancient woodlands, however, have so much more to offer, particularly in the spring before the trees' leafy canopy shades out the woodland floor. In fact there is a race going on where the flowers below have to complete their cycle of growth before they are shaded out by the trees overhead and no longer receive enough sunlight to photosynthesise effectively.

A woodland that is well managed will provide additional intermittent opportunities for plants to grow, flower and set seed. Historically, all English ancient woodlands were coppiced for their products, with just a few trees left to grow to maturity to provide larger timbers for building purposes. Coppicing has the effect of opening up the woodland floor to sunlight for a few years before the coppice regrowth shades it out once more until the next round of coppicing begins. For those few years there will be an explosion of ground flora.

Ancient woodlands are also rather special places because they have not been subjected to modern farming pressures. Indeed, the plant communities have established themselves over hundreds of years during which time they have found areas within the woodland that most suit their needs. They are very unlikely to spread beyond the woodland perimeter because those habitats are unsuitable. Some of these plants are quite special, even though they may not normally be uniquely associated with ancient woodland, because they have become 'marooned' in an intensively managed agricultural landscape so any seeds that might 'escape' the woodland are most unlikely to grow. This is amply demonstrated on the wood bank opposite the Lawshall Swan pub, where ancient woodland plants continue to grow on what was the original woodland boundary before the southern section was bulldozed to make way for cultivation during the 1960s. In effect they are prisoners on the bank and the seeds that they produce have no suitable habitat to spread to. Lack of connectivity to adjacent good habitat is therefore a real issue for some of these plants, while a further problem that they may face in the future is the issue of climate change as they cannot simply move should conditions become unfavourable.

All woodlands have tracks, known as rides, penetrating into them in order to extract coppice and timber products. Rides provide extra opportunities for flowers to establish along the interface between track and woodland. These areas are extremely sheltered and on sunny days can be very warm indeed. A wide variety of insects take advantage of the opportunities that the rides offer in terms of shelter, nectar and larval food plants.

There is no doubt that the best time to visit ancient woodlands for their flora is during the spring months. At this time the vernal or spring flowering species are at their best ahead of canopy closure overhead. The walker will be rewarded with drifts of flowers stretching as far as the trees allow the eye to see. In May bluebells, ramsons or ride-side forget-me-not can provide a haze of colour akin to an impressionist painting. The sight is certainly uplifting and unforgettable, and on any bright sunny morning the woodland positively invites you in to explore its secrets.

Each ancient woodland is distinctive and will have its own composition of ground flora. While some of this woodland may have been in the same place since the trees grew up following the retreat of the last Ice Age, man has had an input in all of them in one way or another. Frithy Wood, for example, is situated at the highest and flattest part of the parish which would have made the growing of arable crops difficult. Indeed, it is possible that Frithy Wood grew from its original size and, while we cannot be sure whether this was in response to extra demand for woodland products, it may well have been because the land was so difficult to drain that crops simply did not thrive. Either way, Frithy Wood is very ancient as the manorial map of 1611 shows. Indeed, the very name 'Frithy' is Anglo-Saxon for wood so we might assume that it has a record as woodland stretching back at least fifteen hundred years. The 1611 manorial map also shows that coppicing management was taking place at that time and doubtless had taken place since time immemorial. The plants associated with Frithy Wood, therefore, have a very ancient pedigree. So what is there that makes a visit to the woodland so worthwhile?

As the cold of winter gives way to spring the brown woodland floor begins to green with the shoots of new life. By mid March a carpet of vegetation is already apparent where previously there appeared to be nothing at all. Large areas of Frithy Wood become carpeted with Wood Anemone (*Anemone nemorosa*), their nodding flowers whitening the woodland floor in their millions. Frithy Wood appears to be quite unusual in this respect, and in a good season the superb displays go some way to compensate for the lack of Bluebells (*Hyacinthoides non-scripta*). The plants are very moisture dependent and in dry springs many

Wood Anemone

Oxlip

of them will be blind (non-flowering) but in a favourable season the display is a sight to behold. By mid summer the leaves will have withered away and the spectacular spring show is but a memory. The Wood Anemone is a good indicator of ancient woodland on the boulder clays of Suffolk

As March gives way to April the pale yellow blooms of the Oxlip (*Primula elatior*) take centre stage. This member of the primrose family has a very restricted distribution and is only found in ancient woodland in South-west Suffolk, North Essex and Cambridgeshire, particularly on the heavy chalky boulder clays left behind by the retreating ice sheets. Superficially it looks like the Cowslip (*Primula veris*), a wayside and meadow plant that has smaller and rather more orange flowers. The Oxlip is Suffolk's 'county flower'. One serious problem that the flowering plant has to contend with is the burgeoning number of deer in woodlands. Whilst deer may look very attractive in the country-side they spend a lot of time browsing in ancient woodland which not only changes the structure of the understorey but also damages the woodland flora. In recent years parts of Frithy Wood have been taken into active coppice management once more and the deer pressure has reduced as each coppice is fenced to exclude them. The Oxlip, along with other flora, has benefited so that these plants are now producing seed to increase their populations. Along the ride edges several other flower species take advantage of the abun-dant sunlight during April and here and there the strong blue spires of Bugle (*Ajuga reptans*) will provide splashes of colour. In bygone centuries it was extremely highly regarded as an effective cure for those suffering from the long-term effects of excessive amounts of alcohol but it was also used as a cure-all.

May is the month when the woodland flora really puts on an interesting display. Orchids are quite irresistible to most people even if they take no interest in any other flowers. In Frithy Wood there are three species which can be readily encountered. Most orchids require a reasonably undisturbed habitat and ancient woodland certainly provides the perfect home for the attractive Early Purple Orchid (*Orchis mascula*). These plants are the 'Long Purples' referred to by William Shakespeare. They were included in the bouquet of

Early Purple Orchid

flowers gathered by Hamlet's tragic Ophelia. Although distinctly purple and tall, the centre of the blooms is splashed with white. In some parts of Frithy Wood these attractive orchids flower in considerable profusion and a visit is very worthwhile just to see these tall 'wands' standing above the surrounding vegetation of Dog's Mercury (*Mercurialis perennis*). This provides the perfect background for the orchid flowers. Dog's Mercury is itself a reliable indicator of ancient woodland sites in Suffolk and at this time of year it carpets the woodland floor in dense deep green profusion.

Another species of orchid that can be found flowering in May is the Twayblade (*Neottia ovata, formerly Listera ovata*). This orchid has a very simple arrangement of two very broad leaves which give it its name. From the centre of the two leaves a tall stem grows which is covered for much of its length in very small green flowers. Some might consider this to be rather a disappointment after the wonderful show of Early Purples, but a closer examination of the flowers reveals their exquisite form, somewhat akin to little angels with outstretched arms. These orchids prefer undisturbed sites and whilst they can be found in a range of habitats they are present in almost all of Suffolk's ancient woodlands.

As spring gives way to summer the Common Spotted Orchid (*Dactylorhiza fuchsia*) can be admired 'lighting up' the ride margins. This is very much an opportunist, appearing quickly where rides have been opened up to allow the sun to bathe the tracks in warmth and light. Elsewhere the woodland canopy is closing in rapidly and more and more light is being excluded. This orchid will grow on any reasonably damp and undisturbed chalky soil and woodland rides provide the perfect summer habitat where this species can grow right up to the ride edges. The plant is easily recognisable with the leaf heavily marked with dark spots, and the delicate pale pink flowers marked with mauve lines and dots which show well against the fast growing greenery of late June and early July.

A very common plant of woodland and hedgerow is Lords and Ladies (*Arum maculatum*). It has various local names including Cuckoo Pint or Pintle. The broad, arrow-shaped leaves appear in early spring and power what looks like the plant's flower spike, along with its protective sheath which is very eye-catching. This sausage-shaped spike is in fact not the flower but an enticement to insects, for it smells of decaying meat. The large pale green sheath that surrounds the 'pintle' protects it from the wind and holds the smell. In addition the plant creates a micro-climate which is slightly warmer than the surrounding woodland and this probably increases the effectiveness of the smell. The flowers are actually below the 'pintle' and can only be accessed by passing through a ring of downward facing guard 'hairs'. Once an insect is below these hairs it is effectively trapped and, in its attempts to get out, walks around and transfers pollen to the stigmas, where the ovaries form a group rather like a small clump of frog's spawn. At night the guard hairs relax and the insect may escape having done its job. Evolutionary processes are really pretty smart in coming up with extraordinary and imaginative ways to ensure successful fertilisation.

Lords & Ladies fruit

Herb Paris

The leaves of the Lords and Ladies, which may be spotted or plain, wither away in the early part of the summer because they can no longer effectively photosynthesise in the dense shade and are therefore redundant, but the plant has achieved what it set out to do. The fertilised ovaries on the lower part of the stem, which is all that remains of the plant, swell and during August they begin to show well on the woodland floor as ripening fleshy red berries. These are extremely poisonous to humans.

One of the most unusual and fascinating plants associated with moist ancient woodland is Herb Paris (*Paris quadrifolia*). As its botanical name suggests it generally has four leaves, although in Frithy Wood plants with three, four, five and six leaves have been recorded. However, four broad leaves are the norm. The name has nothing to do with the capital city of France. The four leaves form two pairs and so, from the Latin, comes 'paris'. The plant, however, is also known as True Lover's Knot, the two pairs of leaves once making it the herb of betrothed couples. From the centre of the four leaves rises a short stem which bears a flower of understated architectural symmetry that defies easy description. The long stamens, which produce the pollen, form a 'crown' around the purple ovary which is surmounted by the stigmas where the pollen germinates. These top the ovary rather like antennae. The flower is so very curious that it deserves close inspection with the result that one is left wondering at the extraordinary diversity of evolution. Following fertilisation a single large blue berry is formed. All parts of this plant are poisonous.

By early June the main floral interest is becoming confined to the rides and glades or newly coppiced areas where sunlight warms and brightens the woodland floor. Among the trees the canopy is already dense enough to shade out everything beneath and the vegetation is fairly sparse. Here and there in a temporary shaft of sunlight a few Early Purple Orchids may complete their flowering, but there will be very little to see and enjoy in terms of flowers from late June onwards.

Hairy St John's-wort

Following many years of abandonment the restoration of management is very much work in progress. However, where the sun shines in the rides and sunny corners in early June it is quite a different story. The tiny blue flowers of Wood Speedwell (*Veronica montana*) and its much larger relative, Germander Speedwell (*Veronica chamaedrys*), Herbs Robert and Bennet (*Geranium robertianum & Geum urbanum*) in pink and yellow, and Creeping Buttercup (*Ranunculus repens*), all brighten the ride sides. In the damper spots the single towering stems of Marsh Thistle (*Cirsium palustre*) can reach upwards to an

Hedge Woundwort

impressive two metres or more. They will hold short sprays of flowers off the stem which attract lots of insects and, much later on in the year, seed eating birds.

From July onwards flowering plants are really confined to the rides and so, of course, are butterflies and other insects. Looking deep into the gloomy woodland from the ride paths there is very little to catch the eye. No flower brightens the shade and no bird call breaks the silence. The habitat has simply become too unwelcoming. Along the rides' margins, however, the strong growing Hedge Woundwort (*Stachys sylvatica*) is putting on a fine display of Burgundy coloured spires at this time of year. It is a rather easily overlooked but not unattractive plant and bumblebees adore it, spending hours foraging around the flower heads. The plant was highly regarded by the ancient Greeks and, as its common name suggests, the plant provided an effective treatment for wounds with the leaves being applied in the form of a soothing and healing poultice. Its botanical name gives a clue as to its woodland habitat although, as its common name suggests, it will also be found along many hedged country lanes. Scientific experiments confirm that the plant contains antiseptic elements and a rub of its leaves produces a wonderfully pungent aroma.

Another plant which will be encountered through July and August with its yellow star-shaped flowers is Hairy St John's-wort (*Hypericum hirsutum*). This is another indicator species of ancient woodland preferring boulder clay soils and is most frequent in the south-western part of Suffolk. There are a number of species of St John's-wort with two others occurring in Frithy Wood but this form, besides being hairy, can be identified by the stalked black dots on the edge of the sepals. The flowers are very attractive to hoverflies and also act as a magnet to pollen beetles on account of their bright yellow colour.

Flowering plants are a key constituent in the diversity of ancient woodlands. Butterflies fluttering along the rides are attracted by the range of flowering plants growing there and, without nectar and pollen, the woodland would be much less attractive to many other insects. Of course, the plants referred to in these pages represent just a few of many that may be encountered on a woodland walk. They have been chosen either because they have a strong affinity with ancient woodland or because they are visually striking and easy to spot. There are many more. For example, Ground-ivy (*Glechoma hederacea*), Selfheal (*Prunella vulgaris*) and Enchanter's Nightshade (*Circaea lutetiana*) all have their own stories to tell. In any event, a visit to Frithy Wood for its plants will always reveal something of interest.

Acknowledgement

Photos provided by Adrian Walters

BUTTERFLIES OBSERVED

Wendy Cooper

Frithy Wood is an example of Lowland Mixed Oak and Ash Wood. It is an ancient woodland which has been coppiced over many centuries, but the coppicing regime fell into decline until recently when Green Light Trust took over the management of the wood. The decline in coppicing resulted in the wood becoming very overgrown and dark, with a fall in butterfly numbers as a consequence.

In this type of mixed woodland, if appropriately managed with structured coppicing giving open glade areas and woodland rides, we would expect to see several species butterflies. The most common and easily seen butterflies are Speckled Wood *(Pararge aegeria)*, Large and Small Whites *(Pieris brassicae, Pieris rapae)*, Gatekeeper *(Pyronia tithonus)*, Ringlet *(Aphantopus hyperantus)* and Meadow Brown *(Maniola jurtina)*. Brimstone *(Gonepteryx rhamni)*, Red Admiral *(Vanessa atalanta)*, Small Tortoiseshell *(Aglais urticae)* and Comma *(Polygonia-album)* can also be present. If a wood is ancient and has the right conditions with tree species such as Hornbeam *(Carpinus betulus)* and Wych Elm *(Ulmus glabra)* growing, rarer butterflies such as Hairstreaks *(Satyrium w-album)*, Silver-washed Fritillary *(Argynnis papkia)* and White Admiral *(Limenitis Camilla)* can also be found.

Comma

Speckled Wood

Starting in 2013, Green Light Trust has begun to coppice Frithy Wood, and has also felled larger trees and shrubs to widen the woodland rides, create glades within the wood. This has resulted in the wood becoming much more butterfly friendly, providing the sunny open spaces where butterflies thrive. There is also an area of Wood Pasture adjacent to the managed area of Frithy Wood which provides a habitat for butterflies such as Meadow Brown, Large and Small Whites, Gatekeeper and Ringlet.

In order to see the impact on butterfly numbers of the woodland work being undertaken a transect through the wood, using the public access path, was monitored from the beginning of April to the end of September 2015. This transect covered various habitats within the wood, and included woodland rides, glades, coppiced areas, denser woodland and the Wood Pasture. Copy of the data collected and transect route is held by the Lawshall Archive Group[1]. Observations during visits to the wood for several years before the coppicing was started had shown that the total butterfly numbers and range of species present reflected the lack of favourable habitat available for them.

Butterfly sightings started off slowly in April with the odd Brimstone and Comma, before the first Speckled Wood and Peacock *(Aiglais io)* appeared on a warm sunny day at the end of April. May brought both male and female Orange-tip *(Anthocharis cardamines)*, together with Large and Small Whites. June saw numbers of Speckled Wood increase, and Meadow Brown started to appear along with a Red Admiral.

Orange Tip

July was a good month, with fair numbers of Meadow Brown and later in the month Ringlet. Large White were prolific, and there were reasonable numbers of Speckled Wood, together with Small Skipper *(Thymelicus sylvestris)* and a Comma. Towards the end of the month good numbers of Gatekeeper emerged, mainly in the newly coppiced area. The highlight of the month, and indeed the year, was a sighting of a White-letter Hairstreak – a butterfly which lives in association with elm trees. This butterfly was seen fairly early in the morning sunning itself low down on brambles, on a woodland path adjacent to the two Wych Elms growing in Frithy Wood.

White-letter Hairstreak

Unfortunately the weather deteriorated in August, but when it was dry enough to visit Frithy Wood there were still Speckled Wood and good numbers of Large White. A few Gatekeeper and Meadow Brown hung on but after a strong show of Peacock at the start of August, their numbers waned. There were also a few Comma along the open rides. September saw most butterflies disappear, but a second flush of Speckled Wood was evident in the wood.

Altogether 14 species of butterfly were seen over the period studied. Although actual numbers present had not been counted previously more species and in overall greater numbers are now being seen.

By and large the numbers of butterflies seen from April to September reflect figures obtained nationally by Butterfly Conservation in their Big Butterfly Count, carried out in July/August 2015.[2] They show an increase in Ringlet, Gatekeeper and Large White; at Frithy Wood we also had good numbers of all these species. Nationally the Count shows a drop in Speckled Wood numbers yet at Frithy Wood reasonable numbers of this butterfly were seen, especially with a second flush in September (after their count took place). The numbers, however, started from a very low base pre-coppicing, when only the odd one was seen.

The most prolific areas for butterfly numbers within the wood were the newly coppiced areas and the Wood Pasture; this is to be expected as these areas benefited from additional light. Speckled Wood are fairly well spread throughout the more wooded areas, while Comma and Brimstone favour the rides.

It is to be hoped that this report will provide a start for further surveys as Green Light Trust continues with its work of coppicing and opening up the woodland rides, more butterflies will take advantage of the improved habitats.

BUTTERFLIES SEEN IN FRITHY WOOD 2015		
Family: Nymphalidae		
1.	SMALL TORTOISESHELL (ST)	*Aglais urticae*
2.	RED ADMIRAL (RA)	*Vanessa atalanta*
3.	COMMA.. (C)	*Polygonia-album*
4.	PEACOCK (P)	*Aiglais io*
Family: Hesperiidae		
5.	SMALL SKIPPER (SS)	*Thymelicus sylvestris*

Family: Pieridae		
6.	ORANGE-TIP (OT)	*Anthocharis cardamines*
7.	SMALL WHITE (SW)	*Pieris rapae*
8.	BRIMSTONE (B)	*Gonepteryx rhamni*
9.	LARGE WHITE (LW)	*Pieris brassicae*
Family: Satyrinae		
10.	SPECKLED WOOD (SWD)	*Pararge aegeria*
11.	GATEKEEPER (G)	*Pyronia tithonus*
12.	MEADOW BROWN (MB)	*Maniola jurtina*
13.	RINGLET (R)	*Aphantopus hyperantus*
Family: Lycaenidae		
14.	WHITE-LETTER HAIRSTREAK (WLH)	*Satyrium w-album*

Acknowledgement

Photographs courtesy of Butterfly Conservation

BATS RECORDED

Nick Sibbett

No recording of bats had taken place in Frithy Wood prior to the survey undertaken first in 2014 and followed up with a second visit in 2015. The surveys were undertaken by Nick Sibbett, Suffolk Bat group member and chair of a local community woodland group, Woodland Ways. In both years, the surveys were combined with a bat walk for Green Light Trust affiliated group members, on one evening in August from sunset for a couple of hours. Participants used a variety of bat detectors, including heterodyne types to listen to bat calls and an Anabat SD2 bat detector (2014) and an EchoMeter Touch bat detector (2015) to record calls. In 2014 an Anabat SD2 bat detector was also left attached to a tree four metres above ground for three days to record bats flying past.

There are 18 resident species of bat in the UK, with 13 species having been recorded from within Suffolk. Three, or possibly four, species have been found so far in Frithy Wood. The commonest two species of bat in the UK are also the ones most commonly found in Frithy Wood. These are Common pipistrelle (*Pipistrellus pipistrellus*) and Soprano pipistrelle (*Pipistrellus pygmaeus*), which are so similar they were once thought to be the same species and were only recognised as different species around 20 years ago. There are slight differences when the bats are seen in close-up: the Common pipistrelle has darker fur on its face, and the two bats have different patterns of veins in part of the wings. One of the UK's rarest bats, the Barbastelle (*Barbastella barbastellus*), has also been found in Frithy Wood, recorded as it briefly flew past some surveyors holding a bat detector in the wood in August 2014. The fourth bat to be possibly recorded was from the *Myotis* group of bats. A very faint call was recorded in August 2014 by a bat detector left unattended in the wood, which could well have been from a *Myotis* bat, although exactly which type of *Myotis* bat is impossible to tell because they all make very similar calls.

All UK bats eat insects, with different bats feeding in slightly different ways and catching different species and sizes of insect. Most insects are caught and eaten in mid-air, though bats sometimes find it easier to hang up to eat larger prey. All bats have very big appetites relative to their size because flying uses up lots of energy. A Common pipistrelle can eat over 3,000 tiny insects in a single night.

Common Pipistrelle by Hugh Clark

Barbastelle by Hugh Clark

Soprano Pipistrelle by Dave Short

Bats are not blind and can see almost as well as humans. To fly and hunt for insects in the dark, they use a remarkable high frequency system called echolocation. Echolocation works in a similar way to the sonar used by dolphins and submarines. Bats make calls as they fly and listen to the returning echoes to build up a picture of their surroundings. They can tell how far away something is by how long it takes the sounds to return to them. The bat can also tell the size and shape of the object, and which way it is moving, which are key to catching flying insects.

The Common pipistrelles and Soprano pipistrelles seen in Frithy Wood were all hunting insects when they were recognised. They were flying to and fro along wide tracks, or circling over coppiced glades. These areas are perfect for hunting because natural woodland produces a lot of flying insects, such as midges, moths, beetles and flies, and the trees provide good boundaries to their echolocation. The bats know exactly where they are, with a good mental map of their surroundings, but do need trees, hedges or other features to provide a surface off which to bounce their echolocation calls. Without anything to echolocate to, bats are completely lost, as though lost in a fog, and so it is rare to see most bats crossing wide open spaces.

The Common pipistrelle bats' and Soprano bats' roost site is unknown. Each species may have a roost in a tree in the wood, or may roost in one of the buildings in Lawshall village. It is likely that bats roost in more than one Lawshall property and so the bats in Frithy Wood may have come from one of these. Pipistrelles, like other bat species, often use multiple roosts in a year. Male bats live alone or in small loose groups and can switch roost locations every few days. Female bats gather in colonies to give birth, but outside the maternity period female bats also switch roosts regularly. Male bats are rarely present in maternity colonies and play no part in rearing the youngsters. Building roosts and tree roosts are all used by bats in each year. Even if the maternity colony is in a nearby building, trees in Frithy Wood are likely to be used by males and females of these species at some point in their life cycle.

The Barbastelle was recorded in the wood briefly, when it flew straight past on its way to somewhere rather than flying around foraging. Barbastelle bats have a pugnacious appearance with their ears joined together across the top of their head and a rather predatory face. They are medium sized for a bat, and feed on flying insects. Unlike most bats, Barbastelles fly deep within woodland, manoeuvring carefully between trees where other bats can't fly. They also roost almost exclusively in trees, often just under a flap of loose bark, with only a handful of colonies living in barns. Barbastelle bats are one of Britain's rarest mammals, with breeding sites very scarce indeed. Improvements in bat detector technology in the last ten years have made it easier to find these little animals in flight, but finding roosts is very difficult. The timing of the 2014 recording, not too long after sunset, suggests that the Barbastelle could well be roosting in Frithy Wood at least on some occasions, in a hollow within a tree trunk or branch, or even under a loose flap of bark that is bigger than A4 size.

The very faint call, possibly from a *Myotis* bat, could well have been from a Natterer's bat (*Myotis nattereri*), which is one of the commonest within the *Myotis* group. It is a woodland bat and, as well as hunting flying insects, it also catches invertebrates from the ground. Analysis of droppings from Natterer's bats has found remains of centipedes, woodlice and other ground living species which certainly weren't caught in flight. Natterer's bats have also been known to fly up to a large spider's web stretched between trees, hover and pick the spider out of the centre, then fly backwards and away with the food item.

Brown long-eared bats (*Plecotus auritus*) have not yet been definitely recorded in Frithy Wood, but could well be present as this is a relatively common species. The Brown long-eared bat is sometimes called the whispering bat, because its echolocation is very quiet and short range, which is why bat detectors rarely record it. This species catches a large proportion of its prey from tree leaves. It is thought to be able to hear the movement of a caterpillar or the rustling wings of a resting moth without needing to use echolocation, another reason why it is so hard to detect.

Further study is likely to uncover more of the mysteries about the bats in Frithy Wood. And as we move into the future, retaining all the trees with hollows, cracked branches and loose bark, as well as continuing the coppice cycle, will ensure the wood continues to support these enigmatic and special animals.

Acknowledgement

Photographs supplied by the Bat Conservation Trust

COMMON BIRD CENSUS

Grenville Clarke

Local volunteers have been recording breeding birds in the woodland since 1976. In spring 2013 and 2015 surveys were undertaken and have been compared with a 1981 survey[1] which has been used as a 'baseline' for the data collected. The survey results for key species were also reviewed against national and regional bird population trends.[2],[3]

Birds, being near the top of the food chain, are useful indicators of the health and biodiversity of differing habitats in the woodland. With this in mind it was felt that, with the reinstating of coppicing, there was a good opportunity to see if changes had taken place to breeding bird populations and their distribution within the wood. External factors can also have a big influence on populations and these are discussed below.

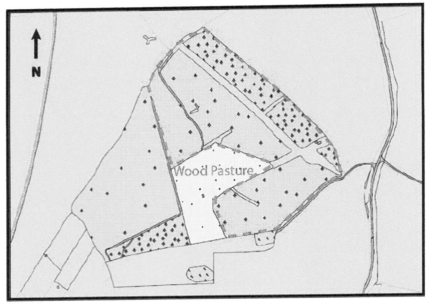

Outline of Frithy Wood: the red lines enclose GLT Ownership.

Woodland Survey Methodology

The Common Bird Census (CBC) method was followed. This was developed by the British Trust for Ornithology (BTO) in the 1960s to measure breeding bird numbers by recording territories of singing males in the spring. The CBC was used nationally until 2000 when it was superseded by the Breeding Bird Survey (BBS); results for both are comparable. The CBC survey method has always been used in Frithy Wood.

The recording technique is to identify, mainly through birdsong, the territories of individual birds and plot them onto detailed maps. Using different observers working separately good coverage was obtained over the breeding season from late March to June. The data was brought together at the end of the survey and individual species' territories were mapped. Data from the 1981 survey was also compared with that obtained during the 2013 and 2015 breeding seasons.

Since January 2013 a new coppicing programme has been in place and areas covering much of the GLT part of the wood will be cut in rotation over the coming years.

Objectives

The work sought to establish whether or not reinstating the annual coppicing regime would improve the numbers of breeding birds within the woodland and to see how quickly coppiced areas are populated. Findings were compared with other data collected in the UK.

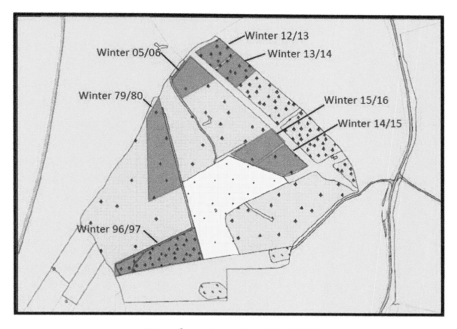

Map of coppice regime since 1996

External Factors

A number of factors which can have a bearing on bird populations were considered.

Climate change. Climate change has had a detrimental effect on migration routes for a number of trans-Saharan migrants. It has also brought about changes in the distribution and onset of egg laying dates for both resident and migrant visitors.

Weather. Local temperatures and rainfall can affect breeding success in the spring which will result in a drop in population numbers the following year. Long cold spells in the winter can cause high mortality levels in birds like Wren and Dunnock.

Woodland management. In the 1960s research was undertaken by the Nature Conservancy Council which confirmed that coppiced woodland with standard trees provided one of the most diverse habitats for wild birds, insects, plants and mammals. The key finding was that coppiced woodland reached its prime biodiversity value at around 6 to 10 years after being coppiced. The coppicing regime in Frithy Wood had lapsed, which may have led to a decline in biodiversity and contributed to dwindling numbers of breeding birds. The history of the Frithy Wood coppice regime is shown in Figure 2 on Pg. 45.

Woodland grazing by deer. Unprotected coppiced areas in Frithy Wood are at risk through overgrazing by deer. The most recent compartment coppiced by the previous owners was protected and the regeneration was successful. All the recently coppiced areas in the wood have deer fencing around them which will remain until re-growth has reached a stage when it is less vulnerable to deer grazing.

Survey Results

The following chart shows the raw data on population changes of twelve species of birds that have bred in the woodland. The 1981 data has been used as a baseline; however, bird populations throughout much of England prior to this were much higher. In the 1960s the increased use of agrichemicals together with an increased emphasis on food production led to a sharp decline in bird numbers. Since 1970 research shows that woodland bird populations have declined by 25% in England; fragmentation of natural habitats and rising temperatures have also contributed to this decline.

The 1981 survey shows 100 territories held by 12 key woodland species. It is pleasing that the total number of territories held in 2015 was 85, which is 26 up from 2013. The key question is whether this is due to the increased woodland management or is it just part of wider population trends and/or other external factors?

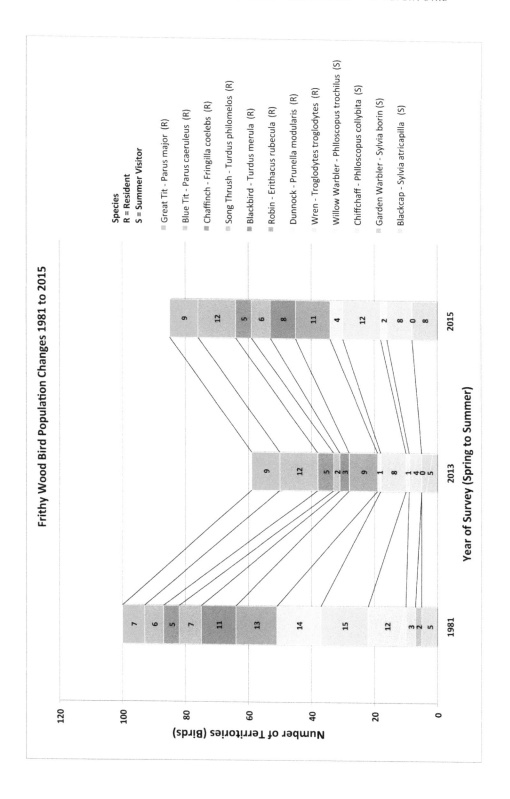

Frithy Wood Bird Population Changes 1981 to 2015

Species
R = Resident
S = Summer Visitor

Great Tit - Parus major (R)
Blue Tit - Parus caeruleus (R)
Chaffinch - Fringilla coelebs (R)
Song Thrush - Turdus philomelos (R)
Blackbird - Turdus merula (R)
Robin - Erithacus rubecula (R)
Dunnock - Prunella modularis (R)
Wren - Troglodytes troglodytes (R)
Willow Warbler - Philloscopus trochilus (S)
Chiffchaff - Philloscopus collybita (S)
Garden Warbler - Sylvia borin (S)
Blackcap - Sylvia atricapilla (S)

Review of Key Species

Great Tit (Resident)

The map below shows that the population of this bird has remained quite stable over the years and reflects a regional trend with a small increase in numbers. Its distribution pattern within the wood has changed very little. Like many birds they are laying eggs about 11 days earlier than in the past – this is attributed to climate warming.

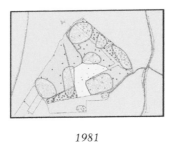

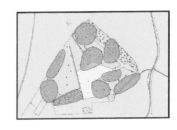

1981   *2013*   *2015*

Blue Tit (Resident)

The Blue Tit population has doubled from 1981 and remained constant from 2013 to 2015 with twelve breeding sites. The territories are now evenly spread over the woodland and it would seem that they have filled most of the preferred breeding location. The regional figures for 1995 to 2013 showed an increase in breeding numbers of 18%.

Chaffinch (Resident)

The 1981, 2013 and 2015 records show that numbers have increased in the wood to five sites. Nationally until the 1970s the population had been declining, but an increase followed until about 2005 when a sharp decline took place due to a fungal infection, Trichomoniasis, which was discovered to be killing both Chaffinches and Greenfinches.

Song Thrush (Resident)

Nationally since the 1990s populations of Song Thrushes have grown by 10%, but regionally they have declined by 12%. Our maps below show Frithy Wood has bucked the trend; in 2015 there was just one territory less than in 1981, which is remarkable as over a 46 year period there has been a decline of 57% in the national population.

  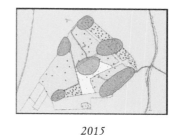

1981   *2013*   *2015*

Blackbird (Resident)

There has been an increase in the population from 2013 to 2015 to eight sites. This is at odds with the national picture of a long term decline until the 1990s, followed by partial recovery until 2005, followed by a decline again. The biggest decline has been in deciduous woodland.

Robin (Resident)

Robin numbers have increased from 2013 to 2015 and this is reflected in regional data. It is rewarding to see on our maps that singing males are now more widely distributed throughout the wood.

Robin - by Neil Calbrade

 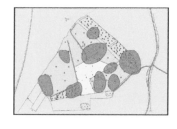 

1981 *2013* *2015*

Dunnock (Resident)

The maps below show large drops in the population which can almost certainly be attributed to the increase in deer numbers in the wood since the 1980s. Damage to the understorey, reducing feeding and nesting opportunities, has had a major effect on this species. The one bird recorded breeding in the woodland pasture might be due to increasing bramble growth at the base of standards.

Dunnock - by Jill Pakenham

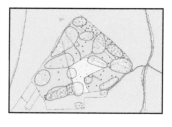 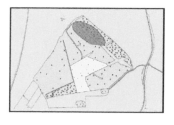 

1981 *2013* *2015*

Wren (Resident)

This is another species that likes dense cover to forage in and seems to have benefited from the reduction of deer grazing along with coppicing. It can be seen that two new territories have been established in 2015 in coppice which is 10 years and two years old. The latter area was deer fenced. The Wren has the highest population of breeding birds in the UK – 1 out of 10 birds recorded are Wrens, this is reflected in our records.

 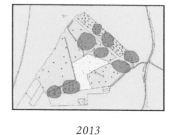 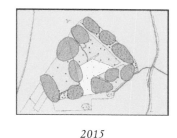

| 1981 | 2013 | 2015 |

Willow Warbler (Migrant)

This species has been in rapid decline nationally since the 1960s and this continues today. However, it is a surprise that populations in Scotland are unaffected by this trend. As can be seen below we have managed to attract two males to the recently coppiced areas, which is very rewarding.

Willow Warbler - by Moss Taylor

1981	*2013*	*2015*

Chiffchaff (Migrant)

Findings for Frithy Wood reflect national figures with a widespread increase in the population from the mid 1980s. Once again the newly coppiced areas have been occupied.

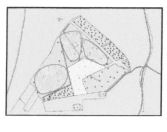

1981	*2013*	*2015*

Garden Warbler (Migrant)

The situation at Frithy Wood reflects the strong decline in populations in southern Britain, and there were no breeding records in either the 2013 or 2015 surveys. In the north and west of the UK numbers are holding up.

Blackcap (Migrant)

Nationally numbers have been increasing. Since the 1970s the population in Frithy Wood has increased to six pairs and they are showing a preference for coppiced areas.

Blackcap - by Mike Dawson

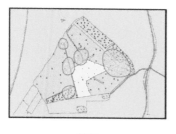

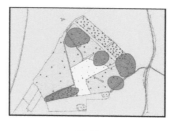

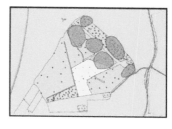

1981   *2013*   *2015*

Checklist of all breeding birds in Frithy Wood 2015

Common Buzzard	Wood Pigeon
Green Woodpecker	Great Spotted Woodpecker
Goldcrest	Blue Tit
Great Tit	Coal Tit
Marsh Tit	Long-tailed Tit
Chiffchaff	Willow Warbler
Blackcap	Nuthatch
Treecreeper	Wren
Starling	Blackbird
Song Thrush	Mistle Thrush
Robin	Dunnock
Chaffinch	Yellowhammer

Gains and Losses since 1981

Gains – Buzzard

Losses – Moorhen, Lesser Spotted Woodpecker, Turtle Dove, Garden Warbler, Spotted Flycatcher and Jay

Non breeding areas in the wood

By recording the distribution of breeding sites throughout the wood two areas which have very few breeding records were seen. One area within the adjacent part of the wood, not owned by GLT, is very low in numbers although it does have Great Spotted Woodpeckers breeding in the mature trees. The second is the area around the pond which is devoid of breeding birds and seems a good candidate for coppicing in the coming season. Surveying prior to management highlights those compartments which are most in need of attention and would quickly provide positive results for breeding birds.

Winter birds

The work concentrated on breeding birds but it should also be remembered that the wood hosts roosts of Redwings and Fieldfares, sometimes in large numbers, as well as flocks of Siskin. Also, one or two Woodcock overwinter in the wood. It is well worth a stroll at dusk to see if these winter visitors are using the wood.

Conclusions

It is very evident that the reduction in deer numbers has resulted in a revival of bird numbers. The fencing of the four newly coppiced areas has restricted the area of easily browsed regenerating shoots and perhaps the increase in footfall has also contributed to deer not finding Frithy Wood such an attractive feeding ground. Other research has shown that over-grazing by deer has a negative effect on woodland flora and fauna.

Global warming has also had an effect on a number of migrant species breeding in Frithy Wood, especially Willow and Garden Warblers. Many birds are breeding sooner than before and some migrants are arriving back sooner, while others like Chiffchaff and Blackcap are overwintering. The GLT management regime will continue to improve the wood and this will enhance the chances of survival for those birds that have opted to breed in Frithy Wood.

Overall the survey team is pleased that our data shows the progress made in reviving this woodland for bird numbers; we believe that the coppicing efforts are helping to improve the biodiversity of Frithy Wood and that it will continue to improve as more compartments are brought into management.

It is hoped that the work carried out with Frithy Wood will encourage others to take up the challenge of bringing many neglected woods in Suffolk and elsewhere back into good health.

Finally, the wider value of Frithy Wood is enhanced by neighbouring land owners who have created or maintained the wildlife corridors such as field margins, set-aside areas and hedgerows that connect the wood with the surrounding landscape and thereby improve the wildlife and aesthetic value of the wood.

Acknowledgements

The recorders for the survey were Cliff Cooper, Clive Grimwood, Trevor Kerridge, John Hobbs and Grenville Clarke.

Special thanks to Eamonn Driscoll, a volunteer and participant in the Restoring the Repertoire programme, who compiled the maps.

The BTO kindly provided the photographs.

EDUCATION AND SKILLS

Tom Brown

The very fact that Frithy Wood still remains today, albeit reduced in size, is testament to its importance for the community that surrounds it. Historically the products and timber that came from the woodland would have been the most significant factor in its importance to people. Inevitably, over time, the neighbouring community became less reliant on these resources. Unfortunately this process also disconnected people from the woodland. The management practices and associated skills which made the woodland such a species and habitat rich environment also ceased, the effects of which have already been outlined in previous chapters. Over recent years GLT's association with Frithy Wood has enabled the community to reconnect with the woodland. Education has been the key driver for this reconnection, particularly through the link to the local primary school which abuts the south western corner of the woodland. This stemmed from GLT's long term commitment to Forest School training, which Hana Jones has been involved with from the beginning.

Forest School Training

Hana Jones, Forest Schools Tutor

We are standing in the field at the boundary edge of Frithy Wood. A group of people made up of Primary School Teachers, Teaching Assistants and Early Years' practitioners, perhaps a Head teacher or an Education Advisor, and many who are also parents. They are all aware that most of our children are spending very little time outdoors in nature in the way that so many of us did when we were young. The effect of this is now showing up in their behaviour and their health. The group is committed to bringing the children they work with outdoors on a regular basis to give them the freedom and space to develop a deeper connection with the natural wild world around them.

Under an ancient oak tree the group pauses and is reminded of a common social tradition that we never just walk into a neighbour's house but always stop to knock on the door to ask if we might come in to visit. The same applies to entering woodland; it is, after all, home for many other beings who are accustomed to the woods being quiet, peaceful and undisturbed by human visitors. The group asks this old oak tree at the boundary edge, "Grandmother Oak, may we come in to play please?" We wait for a response. It takes time – the answer has to come up from the roots to the branches and we know that trees move slowly... Some may say it was the wind, but there is always a response; even on the stillest of days a leaf moves, a branch sways and some even say they can feel something in their own hearts that they know means, "Yes, of course – you are welcome to come in here!"

At Green Light Trust Forest School training is run as an experiential process so that the adult practitioners can have a similar experience to that which their children will get. This has been done in Frithy Wood since 2003 with permission from the previous owners. Every student who attends Forest School training at Green Light Trust gets to experience the magic of this ancient woodland and the impact this incredible place has on their spirits and their overall health and well-being. Many of the students remark on the fact that they had not stopped and just sat in nature before and that the sense of timelessness during the outdoor element of their training was refreshing and restorative. They learn a wide range of practical skills to utilise in their own Forest School sessions such as fire lighting, knot tying, shelter building, bug hunting, tree climbing, whittling and much more. Alongside the practical skills they delve deep into learning theories, child development and how to keep everyone safe enough so the children can experience taking risks and overcoming any fears.

One to one training.

GLT tutors training Forest School Leaders

The ethos that underpins good Forest School practice involves enabling child-centred learning to take place in an outdoor environment; the children lead the way and the adults follow their lead, walking beside them, joining in with their play and supporting them to achieve what they have decided is important to do on that day, in that moment. Children have an innate desire to learn and in the outdoor environment learning takes place without any pressure to do so through the child's natural passion to explore and wander in these surroundings and to play in this space. While quietly hiding and waiting to be found during a game of hide and seek, without realising it the children are learning as they watch a bird making a nest, a spider catching a fly or an ant pushing a small piece of food over a long distance. These seemingly small things, that for many of us are fond memories from the sweet and gentle days of our youth, are not available for many children today. Here they are also given the chance to take reasonable risks while playing in the woods – climbing a tree, balancing on a log, swinging from a rope swing, using a saw to cut firewood, cooking over an open fire, telling everyone the story of their day in the woods in the closing circle. Such satisfying activities that make us feel good about ourselves when we persevere and then succeed, are all available for children at Forest School.

The benefits of this way of teaching and learning are that it raises a child's self-esteem and confidence and improves their skills as independent learners and social beings. Connecting with nature helps children, and adults, to understand themselves better; it slows down the mental chatter and any stress responses that come from the need to 'achieve', to fulfil targets, or to 'learn'. The children, and the adults working with them, become happier and healthier as a result. Through training Forest School leaders who will each be taking children outdoors on a regular basis, we aim to help our children grow into resilient, resourceful, confident, self-assured, socially and emotionally aware adults who care about the world they live in. What could be a better legacy to leave the world with?

Forest School Education in Action at Lawshall School

Clare Lamb, Headteacher of All Saints' Church of England Voluntary Controlled Primary School.

Children at All Saints' enjoy a rich diet of outdoor learning through their work as a Food for Life Flagship School, their involvement in the 'From Seed to Tree' programme and their participation in Forest Schools. Forest Schools are an integral part of the school and are part of the educational offer that parents and children value. Such is the school's commitment to developing and sustaining this provision that the school's Head Teacher and Key Stage One Leader have both gained their Level 3 Forest Schools qualification and this year the school will fund their newly appointed Year 5 teacher to gain their Level 3 accreditation. This will ensure that Forest Schools is embedded through the school in each Key Stage, enabling all pupils to have equal and sustained access to outdoor learning throughout their time at All Saints'.

Forest School sessions take place in Frithy Wood, an ancient woodland and Site of Special Scientific Interest, which children access by crossing a meadow behind the school grounds. The school has use of a designated area of woodland complete with its own fully equipped Forest Schools shed. The school has an agreement with the local landowners, in conjunction with Natural England, on the frequency of use of the woodland in order to minimise the risk of site degradation and to allow the site to regenerate between sessions. The Forest

Children off to Frithy Wood to collect seeds to plant in tree nursery.

School site comprises of a base camp, with logs for the children to gather on at the start and end of the session and to participate in adult supported activities such as whittling and using hand saws and drills. The site is bounded with marker tape and all children have a clear understanding that they are safe within the tape as it has been risk assessed and checked.

Children from All Saints' begin their relationship with Frithy Wood and Forest School in their Reception Year and continue to build upon this each year as they progress through the school. This enables the children to build upon their skills and to adapt how they use and experience the woodland as they develop and mature. Each year opportunities are provided so that the older children act as 'forest leaders' to younger pupils, sharing their skills and showing them how to make the most of their time in the woods. Apart from a set of agreed rules, the children know that their time in the woods is their own. Time to explore, be curious, work collaboratively, be independent and to plan their own time.

Staff and pupils at All Saints' School use a set of six learning behaviours that enable children to be effective and engaged learners, and that permeate all aspects of school life: stickability, creativity, independence, cooperation, motivation and curiosity. During each session children are encouraged to set their own challenges and projects, ensuring that they use their learning behaviours. Children are leaders of their own learning in the woods, with adults acting as facilitators and enablers but never directing or influencing what children choose to do. Such an approach ensures that children are encouraged to become independent and resourceful in their learning, which is something that they successfully transfer to their learning within school.

The Forest School approach supports and enhances all aspects of the curriculum, particularly Personal and Social Education. Children are encouraged to set boundaries and rules for the group, to negotiate and to appreciate the importance of developing an understanding of safety through risk assessment. Children's spiritual, moral, social and cultural education is enhanced by their Forest School sessions, with time to experience awe and wonder of the changing seasons and developing a sense of enjoyment and fascination in learning about themselves, others and the world around them.

Case Study 1

The move from the enclosed space of an indoor classroom to an open, active learning space empowers children who can struggle with formal learning. A child with ASD/ ADHD* who displayed behavioural difficulties when in school was able to thrive in the outdoor environment and within the ethos of Forest School. He chose to spend time on his own, avoiding collaborative tasks but instead engaging in self-chosen projects in which he displayed high levels of concentration and manual skills. The pressure that he experienced in working within a confined classroom space within school was immediately

* Autism Spectrum Disorder/Attention Deficit Hyperactivity Disorder

alleviated in the woods. Through time he enjoyed sharing his skills with others and as a result built positive relationships with his peers. When asked about his reasons for enjoying Forest Schools, he confidently articulated, "There are no walls, no ceilings and no corridors, just space to think".

Case study 2

In a Forest School Session with children in Key Stage Two and Reception, older children from Year 3, with a wealth of experience of Forest School and associated skills, take on leadership roles for the session. They have spent the previous week creating resources and setting up the woods in preparation for the younger children. They work with small groups and individuals modelling a range of activities including den building, hunting for mini beasts and making bows and arrows. It is interesting to see that the older children adopt a coaching role, asking questions and giving prompts rather than directing and leading.

Clare Lamb

Two Year 3 boys are seen advising a group of younger boys in how to make a den. They organise them with tape measures and hard hats, showing them how to measure the wood so that it will make the right size den. At this point they step back and only step in to support when the logs are too heavy to lift.

The benefits of the Forest School approach, which develops independent, resourceful and creative learners, are fully embedded within learning across the school and across the curriculum.

'From Seed to Tree' in Frithy Wood – How it Started

Ric Edelman, joint Founder of Green Light Trust

This section describes the start of children's activities in Frithy Wood. Working with pupils from All Saints' Primary School in Lawshall, it outlines the evolution of the 'From Seed to Tree' programme and Frithy Wood's importance in this process.

A class of 5 and 6 year olds are merrily tottering about under a stand of oaks. The hazy October sun filters through the yellowing autumnal leaves and the children's eyes are glued to the ground, searching for acorns.

It's the mid-1990s and this is the forest pasture on the edge of Frithy Wood. Nigel and I are leading a Green Light morning for Forest for Our Children (FOC), inaugurated in 1993 by William Takaku, chief of the Flying Fox clan from Papua New Guinea.

For the first couple of years, we only involved Year 4 who planted saplings in our new community woodlands. However, the enthusiasm of pupils and teachers alike soon led us to devise what became the 'From Seed to Tree' programme involving all four year groups.

Hence today's first visit to Frithy Wood!

After a story under the trees and a chance for the children to hop about as rabbits and squirrels in the shaggy willow herb and sunlit grasses, we ferry them to the new tree nursery at Lawshall Green, to plant their acorns and offer a rainforest prayer to help them grow. These same children will return next year to tend their seedlings and, in Year 4, dig them up and transplant them in Golden Wood.

In later years, we invited the neighbouring primary schools at Hartest and Cockfield to join the programme, and a greatly expanded band of little foragers continued to visit Frithy Wood each autumn. Eventually, we encouraged the other schools to develop their own tree nurseries, though Lawshall Year 1 still continued its annual acorn hunt until there was no room for any more saplings in Golden Wood.

The programme was sadly missed, and just recently, the Year 1 foragers have been out again in the forest pasture, now planting their acorns in a nursery built at the school. Only a stone's throw away stands the inaugural tree planted by William Takaku – when some of the current children's mums and dads were pupils at the school!

During the early FOC years, we worried that the older Lawshall children and teenagers had no connection to the project, so every term we offered an outdoor activity to the village youth club known as the drop-in centre.

These included visits to Frithy Wood to learn tracking. Here on a couple of summer evenings we split into small groups and, among the brambles and dog's mercury, sought out and followed the tracks of deer and badgers. On one occasion, dusk was already falling when we reconvened to leave; a wind had blown up and the boughs around us were swaying and creaking while the last calls of Blackbird and Chiffchaff filled the air. One 13 year old boy who had never been in the wood before, stood mesmerised by the magic. "Can't we stay all night?" he begged. "I want to stay here forever!"

On other occasions we made survival shelters and the youth worked arduously in pairs, fully absorbed. At the end of the session the adults walked around and visited the shelters. Inside each, we found the gleeful inhabitants cosily squatting or curled up under blankets of dead leaves. Again, as the first stars appeared, they pleaded to stay all night, and vowed to return to look after their new and cherished forest homes.

Heritage Lottery Funded Education and Skills Development

At the end of 2012 GLT secured funding from the Heritage Lottery Fund to purchase 21 acres of Frithy Wood. Education and learning traditional skills were the main focus of this £485,000 project. The project used methods of engagement influenced by Forest School practice but with more prescribed learning outcomes, engaging mainly with marginalised and disadvantaged individuals, along with a programme aimed at contextualising the mainstream curriculum in a woodland setting with school groups.

As with the Forest School activities outlined above, a large proportion of the education delivered as part of the 'Restoring the Repertoire' project was informal and focused on supporting individuals to develop their resilience and most importantly self-confidence to enable them to move their lives forward, while at the same time carrying out the woodland tasks required to bring Frithy Wood back into active management. As the project progressed, however, the emphasis shifted to more formal education programmes, leading to qualifications. This evolved organically as it became clear that having academic currency was an important factor in enabling individuals to progress beyond their engagement with this project.

GLT is an Awarding Bodies Consortium (ABC) Awards approved provider centre. This enables us to deliver Practical Environmental and Conservation Skills (PECS) courses from entry level up to level 2. One of the first groups to benefit initially attended a Woodland Alternative Curriculum Engagement (ACE) programme. In 2013 fourteen Year 10 students, in two groups, attended six ACE sessions in the wood. During the course of this programme and from feedback received, it quickly became clear that a number of students were flourishing because of the sessions and wanted to learn more about how the woodland was being managed. This group consisted predominantly of pupils who had been identified as lower academic achievers; having been removed from optional subjects at school, they were working towards a personal and social development qualification at the school, and none were predicted to achieve five A*-C grades at GCSE. Without the requisite grades at GCSE these students would normally progress on to a yearlong level 1 programme at college, prior to starting their desired level 2 vocational course. In order to avoid this, ten of these students returned to GLT during their Year 11 studies. Attending for half a day every other week for the whole year, the students worked towards an ABC level 1 PECS award. All of the students achieved this award, and three progressed directly on to a college course following Year 11.

The significance of working towards a qualification goes beyond the simple achievement of a qualification required for a specific job role. It can also provide motivation for individuals to realise how far they have progressed and gain confidence from achieving something tangible. Throughout the three year project additional opportunities were identified to formalise the education that was being delivered. Working with partner organisations, GLT was able to deliver elements of qualifications, which students on the programme were already studying for. A good example of this was a Sustainability and Team Working unit studied by young people on the Young Futures programme. This supported the course they were already following at West Suffolk College, designed to engage those Not in Education Employment or Training (NEET).

Everyone who attended a programme as part of the project learned about woodland management, its relevance and the theory behind the work. It was vital to interpret the work for all participants, but especially so when trying to motivate disengaged individuals who need to see the importance of what they are being asked to achieve. This was not such an issue for the programme which engaged with volunteers from the 60 community wild spaces that GLT had helped to establish across East Anglia. These volunteers were invited to Frithy Wood where they learned about different elements of woodland management, history, archaeology and traditional craft skills. The intention was to impart knowledge and skills which the participants could take back and share with their own communities.

At the beginning of the project the Woodland Heritage Education Active Learning (HEAL) programme was initially designed to allow groups from local schools, predominantly at Key Stage Four, to use the woodland as a way of contextualising their science learning. As the project progressed it quickly became apparent that this approach needed to be modified, as many of the teachers lacked the specific knowledge required to make effective use of this resource. As a result, GLT identified specific elements of the GCSE science curriculum, as well as the A-level Biology and Environmental Studies curriculum, which could benefit from the woodland context. This enabled GLT to engage with additional schools to access the woodland, and an education leader constructed a day with a complementary range of activities allowing the students to carry out some practical tasks, such as fire lighting to boil a Kelly Kettle for their tea break, whilst at the same time learning about the woodland and the area of the curriculum they were addressing that day. A good example of one of these activities was second year A-level students carrying out straight line transect surveys in an area of the woodland that had been coppiced. This enabled them to improve practical skills whilst learning about the process of secondary succession in woodland. Mr Paul Jackson, Head of Science at County Upper School in Bury St Edmunds, commented: *"Woodland HEAL days enabled our A-level students to develop practical skills, and the experience was invaluable for them to draw on when answering essay questions during their exams"*.

Engaging with school groups can be challenging during exam time due to the time pressures that exist within the national curriculum and this meant that GLT found it difficult to meet the commitment made to HLF to engage more than 500 students during the three years of the project. To address this problem, a new programme was piloted through a partnership with a semi-retired head of science, to engage with Key Stage Three students using the woodland. As a pilot a total of 44 gifted and talented Year 6 students from three middle schools, supported by members of staff from each school and assisted by two science captains from County Upper School, descended upon the woodland. The day began with a tour of Frithy Wood led by two members of GLT staff with the students looking out for wildlife. They were then split into mixed groups from each school and carried out a number of tasks. One group carried out some basic plant surveying while another dressed as animals and plants found in the wood and tried to organise themselves into a food web, with debates such as "what does a Badger eat?" and an Adder asking "who eats me?" A third group cut discs of wood from a tree felled as part of the coppicing works taking place in the woodland, and marked the point on the rings when they were born. They took this away as a memento of their day. As a culmination of the day each of the middle schools were presented with a large disc of wood cut from one of the trees that had been coppiced the previous year; this went back to the school to be labelled with notable events in time linked to their corresponding tree ring. These cross curriculum links enhanced the value of this programme to the schools involved, and the same programme was delivered successfully to a number of other schools in the area.

GLT hopes that the wide range of educational activities taking place in Frithy Wood will continue and increase to provide a wonderful legacy for the future.

EVALUATING THE REPERTOIRE

Tom Brown

This chapter addresses the outcomes of the 'Restoring the Repertoire' project. It describes how they were achieved, and presents the data collected to evidence these achievements. As stated in the Education and Skills chapter, where the delivery model for the project was outlined, all of the work to restore the woodland was carried out by individuals as part of their own restorative or developmental journey. To give a reasonable overview it is sensible to break the impact of the project down into two distinct areas – firstly, the impact on the woodland itself and, secondly, the impact on the people involved in the project. As previously reported, Frithy Wood is a Site of Special Scientific Interest (SSSI), and as such Natural England (NE) is the statutory nature conservation body responsible for overseeing its management. Prior to the start of this project NE had classified the whole woodland as being in unfavourable condition and in decline. As Grenville Clarke has outlined in The Common Bird Census, the bird populations are a very good indicator of the condition of the woodland, with different bird species requiring specific habitats. The data produced from the Common Bird Census surveys clearly indicates the improvement of habitats during this short project, which will continue as long as active management continues.

At the beginning of the project an approved woodland management plan was in place, with felling permissions and a Forestry Commission grant under a Woodland Improvement Grant Scheme. The impact on the woodland would be measured against the implementation of the management plan, and the NE condition status of the woodland. The management objectives of this plan were to:

- develop a 10 to 15 year coppicing regime throughout the wood, coppicing 0.25ha per year; and
- improve biodiversity and protection of the site from overgrazing by deer.

Baseline data from the bird surveys were to be used as a measure of the habitat improvements made to the woodland through the project.

The impact upon the people the project engaged with was measured through a questionnaire delivered to participants, once at the beginning of their programme, and then again at the end. The questionnaire was tailored to each group and, along with a general course feedback questionnaire, was designed to measure the 'distance travelled' by each participant during the course. This method, although relatively subjective, worked well to test the 'softer' outcomes of the engagement, such as confidence and self-esteem. However, it was less effective in testing the physical benefits of this type of work. Participants, some of whom had been sedentary for long periods of time, were now taking part in physical activity outside. In order to test the impact on the individual's physical well-being more rigorous tests, such as resting pulse rate and a sit stand test, could have been implemented. However, this would not have been appropriate for many of the project's participants, and may have created a further barrier to their engagement.

Woodland impact timeline

2013

January, February, March

The project officially began delivery at the beginning of January 2013. Ash dieback disease had been confirmed in the woodland, so a decision to continue with planned coppicing was taken in consultation with the Forestry Commission and Natural England. It was agreed that the impact of doing nothing would be more detrimental in the long run than the feared impact on the regeneration of the ash stools. Working with the first groups, a semi-permanent 'bodging' camp was established using a large tarpaulin, and an old Anderson shelter already in the

Newly felled coppice compartment

wood was moved to the camp as a wood store. The first 0.25ha area was coppiced, although no timber was moved to ride side. Felling licences were not in place to fell any of the oak standards so these were left, leaving areas of the compartment over stood (shaded).

April, May, June

Advice to restrict movement of timber from disease infected sites meant that no timber was extracted from Frithy Wood. Groups, predominantly woodland ACE groups assisted by the first Woodland Rescue group, worked during this quarter to move almost all of the timber ride side. A composting toilet was commissioned and delivered. It was decided that this should be accessible by disabled participants and was commissioned from 'Stix and Stones', an Essex based company who came up with a system that reduced the requirement for a

Compost toilet

long ramp. With this in mind a group of prisoners from Her Majesty's Prison (HMP) Highpoint worked to install a disabled access path from the carpark to the entrance of the woodland, moving 20 tonnes of crushed concrete. Heras fencing was delivered to the woodland to protect the coppice compartment from deer browsing. Ground flora outside the fencing was still under high pressure with no Oxlip flowers surviving to set seed.

JULY, AUGUST, SEPTEMBER

The website for the project went live; this was to be used to help support the woodland trail with individual heritage touchpoints. The work to formalise the trail was carried out, paths were cut to allow movement around the trail, and temporary markers were installed while the copy for the trail markers was created. Deer fencing was fully erected with participant groups, enclosing the first coppice area. Good regeneration was seen on coppice stools not over stood by oaks and a flush of ash seedlings was seen. Unfortunately towards the end of August the majority of the ash seedlings had succumbed to Ash dieback and the coppice stools were also showing signs of dieback; however, the other species in the compartment were showing very good signs of regeneration.

OCTOBER, NOVEMBER, DECEMBER

Coppicing work began in a slightly larger compartment adjoining the first year's coppice block. With a new felling licence in place we were now able to fell some of the standards in this compartment to maintain a 20% canopy coverage. Ride widening works were also approved and these began with the first ride being widened in December.

2014

Entrance to Frithy Wood

JANUARY, FEBRUARY, MARCH

The coppicing and felling of standards continued until completion at the end of March. In addition to the ride widening works, brambles encroaching the rides were cut back using Austrian Scythes with a ditching blade. All markers and the entry sign for the trail were installed by participating groups and a launch of the trail was planned. The main ride and entrance to the woodland became difficult to access due to waterlogging and overuse. A solution was agreed with Natural England which would see timbers buried under the ride to help stabilise it, and work was scheduled to take place in early spring.

April, May, June

The first loads of timber were extracted from the wood by its previous owners – just under 10 tonnes were moved as part of the ten year agreement to provide 100 tonnes of firewood. The rides had dried out sufficiently, the planned work to stabilise the entrance was postponed and working methods changed to reduce the damage to the ride. The second coppice block was completely enclosed with temporary deer fencing which adjoined the previous year's compartment. Work to move the wood from the compartment continued. Poles from the wood were moved to the Foundry, GLT's head office, to build a pole barn.

Heritage touch point

July, August, September

All of the cordwood (a term used to refer to cut and stacked timber to be used as fuel) from the coppice compartment was cleared with some of the larger standards being milled with an Alaskan chainsaw-mill. This timber was used to clad the pole barn at the Foundry and for small scale building projects in the woodland. Ride widening activity began again at the end of September.

Ash poles extracted for sculpture

October, November, December

Coppicing of a third block began in a different area of the woodland. The area chosen had few standards, having previously been an area with elm standards that were lost to Dutch Elm Disease. Ride widening continued, along with the felling of a small glade, 40 metres x 30 metres, at the point where two rides cross in the woodland. It is hoped that this permanently open glade will create valuable habitat for a number of different species in the woodland, particularly *lepidoptera* (butterflies) and *chiroptera* (bats). Surveying of archaeological features of the woodland began with a view to creating a more detailed map of the history of the woodland.

Alaskan saw mill being used

2015

JANUARY, FEBRUARY, MARCH

Newly coppiced compartment

The coppicing of the compartment was completed and participant groups began to erect the temporary deer fencing around it. The process of coppicing with the communities of interest had been developed and honed to enable felling of the trees and stacking of timber and brash in separate piles to make the extraction of timber easier.

APRIL, MAY, JUNE

Ride crossway

All of the timber was cleared to the ride side from this season's compartment, using a recently purchased Arbor trolley, a two wheeled trolley which can be easily pulled by two people. This made the whole process far easier and more efficient, dramatically speeding up the whole process. Over 16 tonnes of timber were extracted from the woodland by the previous owners. This was moved from the ride widening and glade creation areas. The fence surrounding the coppice compartment was completed and early signs of regeneration were very positive.

JULY, AUGUST, SEPTEMBER

There was relatively little activity in the woodland which had any impact on its development during this quarter. The new season's coppice compartment was marked up to begin felling in October.

OCTOBER, NOVEMBER, DECEMBER

Coppicing work in this year's compartment was well underway towards the end of December; however, this did run over into

Widened ride

the New Year with the final coppicing being completed with groups at the end of February. Timber from the woodland was moved to the Foundry and was now dry enough to be used in the woodchip boiler to heat the building. Ride widening works continued, although the gradual reduction in groups working in the woodland towards the end of the project meant that no new projects were started.

At the end of the project Natural England provided the following statement to support the work carried out during the project:

> "Prior to the Green Light Trust taking over management responsibility for part of Frithy and Chadacre Woods Site of Special Scientific Interest (SSSI), this ancient woodland had been in decline for a number of years. It wasn't providing the wealth of woodland wildlife that it should. Surveys carried out concluded that significant deer browsing and little or no active woodland management had impacted on the condition of the woodland resulting in a lack of young seedlings/saplings/understorey or re-generation from coppice stools – all of which affected the scarce and typical flora, insect and bird life that should abound in the wood.

> "The Green Light Trust and its community of volunteers, students and young people has made concerted efforts to address these issues through re-introduction of coppicing, fencing off the newly coppiced areas to protect from deer damage and widening rides to benefit ground flora.

> "These improvements have enabled the status to change from 'unfavourable declining' to 'recovering'. A very positive step forwards."

Impact on people

In this section we will attempt to capture some of the impacts the project had on the participants involved with it. In order to do this, each programme described is individually evaluated.

Young Futures

Target participants	Total participants	Percentage of target
90	107	119%

Engaging almost exclusively with groups from West Suffolk College (WSC), this programme was the first to be delivered in January 2013 with a group of 13 participants split almost equally between males and females working in snowy conditions to start the development of the site. This group erected the tarpaulin in what was to become the bodging area, and this tarp still remains today. The initial Young Futures programme was delivered over a five day period, with an additional summary day the following week. This method of delivery meant that some participants could not attend every session, so for the second course, delivered to an all-male group of six participants in December, the course was

71

Participant practising firelighting

Participant with her spoon

Participant coppicing

Tree Felling to widen ride

delivered one day per week for five weeks. This was a far more effective method of delivery and resulted in all participants attending over 80% of the course. Whilst engaging with WSC, GLT attempted to recruit new partner organisations to this programme. A pilot with the Porch project, an organisation in Hadleigh, was arranged but didn't run as there was insufficient uptake from the young people they work with.

In year two GLT worked with 35 participants, over three cohorts. Two of these courses followed the same model as that developed in year one, with the participants attending one day a week for five consecutive weeks. The participants on this programme, are Not in Employment, Education or Training (NEET), or at risk of becoming NEET young people. The third course in year two worked with a group of students at risk of failing their course at WSC and potentially becoming NEET. GLT delivered a programme that used the woodland and its management to address some of the social issues that were preventing the participants from succeeding. This was very successful, with all of the participants rating the course as either 'good', or 'very good' when surveyed. One hundred per cent of the participants on this programme felt they had a better knowledge of what a woodland environment was and how it was managed.

In the final year four courses were delivered with a total of 53 participants. Numbers for the courses had become consistent as the programme and partnership with WSC developed throughout the project. During the course of the project GLT always delivered an environmental unit to the participants; whilst the qualification the students were studying at the college changed, GLT was able to ensure that the participants had the opportunity to learn about the woodland and why they were carrying out the management tasks, a point which is supported by partner feedback. Anne Hately, a tutor who has brought many of the groups to GLT from West Suffolk College, summarised what this programme has done for some of its participants.

"When we ask the students to complete the college surveys at the end of the year they always mention the Green Light Trust even if we had to drag them screaming in the first place!"

"For the majority of them the big benefit is actually discovering you can enjoy yourself in the woods, and the general feel good factor being outside gives you. Again, they nearly always say how they were shattered and went to bed early on those days and slept really well instead of sitting up all night playing on a computer! From the young mum who had no confidence discovering she could make the most amazing models out of plasticine whilst putting together a model of the Green Light Trust as part of the review of their time there, then, spurred on by her new found talent, presented it to the group and GLT staff. A very big step for her. To the young lady who was definitely not cut out for the class room, but had already held a job down for a year. She had come to us from a Pupil Referral Unit and was constantly at loggerheads with staff. During her time at the GLT she took part in a team building exercise where she took the lead and discovered that her communication skills were excellent and she talked her team to the finish line in complete safety. This realisation got us all thinking that maybe college was not the right place for her but she would be better off doing a qualification whilst working

Fire lighting

and aiming towards being a supervisor and then management. The company she worked for was more than happy to offer her this opportunity."

"There are lots of little stories like this, but maybe the most rewarding is the young man who did not have a direction and was constantly getting into trouble with authority. He actually did two years on this course which is unheard of. His time at GLT, however, made him realise that he enjoyed working outside and enjoyed working with wood. Due to his enthusiasm created by his time at the GLT he managed to get work experience with a local tree surgeon. It is very difficult to get work experience in this field but he did very well, travelling to London and all over the South East during his two weeks. The company had only just taken on an apprentice otherwise that would have been his for the taking. As he had done so well and received an excellent reference he obtained a place on the Traineeship course at the college, even though he didn't have the grades. His interest in forestry and woodworking got him some long term work experience, through Traineeships, in a local company making things from wood. He did really well during his three months' work experience and was offered an apprenticeship."

"Apart from these stories there is the very important aspect of respect for the environment and a week working and learning about the importance of woodlands encourages the young people to re-think about littering, recycling and general respect for their world."

Woodland Minds

Target participants	Total participants	Percentage of target
24	92	383%

Woodland Mind courses had a very slow start with only one delivered in the first year with just four participants. This was a challenging group to engage with as a fractured support network and multiple agencies meant there were no single partner organisations GLT could work with to bring a group of eight or more participants to Frithy Wood. In year two GLT had a far more successful model in place; networking with various referral agencies, we were able to take direct referrals on to the courses, organising collection and drop offs from central locations, with taxi journeys for those unable to meet at these points. This resulted in GLT working with 44 participants across five courses. One of these was a pilot Woodland Mind course, specifically for teenage girls suffering with anxiety and depression issues. Nine girls from King Edward VI School, Bury St Edmunds, attended the course. The pupils were regular or high achievers, who had been identified with low confidence, self-esteem or anxiety issues. Without exception, all the girls said they felt less self-conscious in an all-female group, allowing them to relax and engage more fully with a variety of activities.

"I feel more motivated on the days I come here than going to school. There's not as many people here. It's easier to try things with less people." – A

"When approaching something I'm now more determined because of the sense of achievement." – E

"I'd normally choose to work on my own, but I've learnt there are benefits to working in a group." – E

Green woodworking and socialising

"At the start I was well nervous, but by the end I was really enjoying it. It felt like escaping. This is not usually my thing but I really did enjoy it. Didn't feel like school. Less structured so it felt more relaxed." –P

Six months on when interviewed all the girls reported, without exception, that the course helped them with their confidence and anxiety issues, that being outside was an important factor, that they would have liked the course to be longer, and that they would all do the course again and recommend it to others.

For those participants who really benefited from the adult Woodland Minds courses, there is a pathway on to the GLT's Green

Fire lighting

Care programme, where GLT is able to access personal care budgets to enable an individual to continue attending beyond the original course, usually for one day per week, with some participants attending more. In the final year of the project GLT worked with 40 participants

across four courses; a pattern of interest had been established. Unsurprisingly, it was much easier to fill the courses during the spring and summer months, and therefore GLT decided not to run any course in the final quarter of the year.

The pathway for participants on the course continued to develop with those gaining the most from the programme able to progress on to a Green Care placement with the possibility of further volunteer opportunities.

Preparing camp fire

A good example of this was 'E' who attended a Woodland Minds course in May 2015. Coming from a background of high achievement and responsibility 'E' had been attempting to recover from a severe mental breakdown for over two years. Having tried a number of other provisions to no avail, he was instantly at home in the woods. As the course progressed he relaxed and began to interact with the others on the course. 'E' took up a Green Care place for two days per week; during this time he was able to learn more about green wood working and build his mental and physical resilience. After attending as a mentor on the Woodland Minds course in July 2015 he then worked as a volunteer assistant on the September and October courses. During this time his confidence grew, which in turn enabled him to volunteer on the Woodland HEAL sessions delivered with groups of 25 ten year olds. This was testament to how far 'E' had progressed. To date 'E' is still volunteering with GLT beyond the life of the project, and is now also involved with some office based activities while attending Green Care. It is hoped that during 2016 he will no longer require the Green Care placement, progressing to a strictly volunteer role.

This programme has demonstrated a profound and lasting impact on a relatively small percentage of those attending, with a measurable impact on the health and well-being of a majority of those participating. Progression routes for participants have been demonstrated with Woodland Minds participants progressing on to long term support at GLT and volunteer opportunities.

Woodland Rescue

Target participants	Total participants	Percentage of target
24	45	188%

Preparing stakes for dead hedging

As with all the programmes, year one was a process of creating relationships with referral organisations. In May 2013 the first Woodland Rescue course was delivered in Frithy Wood. This course engaged 11 participants who were in a treatment programme with Open Road in Bury St Edmunds, a partner organisation that GLT had already developed a good working relationship with. Following the course feedback and the team's self-assessment review (SAR) the successes of the course were highlighted and areas for improvement noted for the next course.

In year two, once again working with a group from Open Road, GLT engaged 22 participants across two courses. In addition, GLT also attempted to link with Focus 12, another drug and alcohol rehabilitation provider from Bury St Edmunds. This partnership was less successful as their 10-12 week abstinence based programme already had a very well established agenda and GLT was only able to engage with groups for single days. After carrying out an SAR after the activity it was felt that this was not enough time to meet the objectives set out for this target audience and further work with this group was postponed until the final year of the project.

In year three of the project GLT once again worked with a group of seven participants from Open Road. However, in April 2015 Suffolk County Council switched the recovery services contract to Turning Point; during the transition process, the Woodland Rescue course served as a constant for the participants with all eventually being awarded an ABC Award, PECS qualification at a ceremony held in the wood. This was later reported in the East Anglian Daily Times and Bury Free Press. In this final year Focus 12 launched a secondary treatment programme and as part

Cordwood extracted to ride side

of this GLT offered a pilot project that engaged five participants. This was a fantastic success, being greatly appreciated by all those who attended. All those surveyed at the end of the course stated they felt they knew more about conservation and the woodland while four expressed an interest in attending again.

DH attended a woodland rescue course through Open Road in January 2014.

"I attended the Frithy Wood Project in January 2014. I had just left the Norcas Day Program where I was receiving help with my alcohol problem.

"After I left Norcas I started attending Open Road where I heard about The Green Light Project. I was really interested as I felt I needed more structure, routine, and to be doing something productive.

"At the project there were a group of six or seven people all at different stages of their recovery. I learned about Conservation and to socialise with other people. I learned about team building and really enjoyed getting into the forest with no communication with the outside world. I felt calm and at one with nature while I was there. I made some great friends, learnt new skills and thoroughly enjoyed myself.

I would highly recommend this course!"

Moving timber

This programme has demonstrated support for a large number of participants who are currently in recovery from drug and/or alcohol addiction. The development of the programme has allowed participants to access educational opportunities, increasing their chances of progressing into conservation/land-based training or employment.

Activities for All

Target participants	Total participants	Percentage of target
180	186	103%

Initially this programme had seemed difficult to recruit to. Engaging with local special schools had proved challenging, with a number of the schools feeling that their students would not be able to access the activities on offer. Towards the end of Year One GLT met with Mick Truman, Deputy Head at Priory School in Bury St Edmunds, a Special School with pupils at Key Stages Two, Three and Four. It was agreed that a pilot programme would be delivered, and in September, October and November 2013 GLT worked with 55 students. Activities designed to engage these students as well as challenging them allowed them to enjoy positive experiences in the woodland. Good links with the students' curriculum activities created additional value for the school, with staff from GLT visiting the students to erect bird boxes in the school grounds that they had made during the activities in the wood. This relationship was further strengthened in year two when a further 77 students accessed the activities on offer in the woodland. As these were single day activities, no feedback was gathered from the students. However, there has been feedback from the school, as shown by these comments from Deputy Head, Mick Truman.

Having fun

"Working at Frithy Wood is an ideal location especially for the emotional wellbeing of our students. In the group students who have been experiencing mental health difficulties were able to explore the woods and have time to express their needs in a way not possible in the classroom. This has been especially important for one student in the group. He has said that he enjoys this work and gives a positive report to his parents at the end of the day. All the students have looked forward to the visits each week. I have had better engagement in the learning activities preparing for and writing about this work."

"In the development of the skills you were teaching, the students were able to develop an understanding of their own abilities, esteem and potential for future lives, maybe even

considering careers in this work. The outcomes of this work with you have been so much more than developing basic practical skills."

Towards the end of this year the student highlighted by Mick Truman assisted GLT with a day in the woods for funders and partner organisations. This allowed him to work with some of the other participants from other programmes.

In the summer of year two GLT was able to take one of the students from Priory School on a work experience placement for a week. 'A' had been one of the students who had previously flourished during the activities in Frithy Wood. Although eager and self-assured he struggled to take direction, he did however settle in very well. Working with some of the other groups of vulnerable adults who attend sessions with GLT, 'A' gained confidence and improved his own self-esteem during this work experience week. Following this experience 'A' returned to GLT a year later to proudly announce that he was taking up a place on a course at a local agricultural college.

In year three GLT worked with 54 students. Once again 33 of these were from Priory School. However, GLT also recruited participants from the Centre Academy, East Anglia, working with 21 students in years 10-12 with varying special educational needs. Activities were similar to those developed to work with the students from Priory School, although these students attended for four days, delivered over four consecutive weeks. This allowed the introduction of camera traps, which enabled the staff to highlight the fauna in the woodland, along with longer term projects less suitable for single day engagements.

Towards the end of year three GLT was able to use funding from this programme to deliver a five week course working with adults with learning disabilities, allowing them to experience the woodland and carry out activities similar to those which the young people from the special schools enjoyed. Four vul-

Lunch time

nerable adults attended this course and, as can be clearly seen from the pictures, gained a lot from the interaction. All of these participants expressed an interest in progressing on to GLT's long term programme, Green Care. Unfortunately only one participant was allowed funding from social services. This is an area where GLT needs to concentrate some attention so that funding can be found to provide continuity.

This programme has allowed children, young people and vulnerable adults to access the woodland whilst learning about it and carrying out activities they would most likely never have had the opportunity to do. Progression has been achieved for some of the participants within GLT as well as to further education (FE) provision. These participants are amongst those least likely to engage with our natural heritage, such as Frithy Wood, had the project not existed.

Woodland ACE

Target participants	Total participants	Percentage of target
36	80	222%

This programme had already been piloted and had an established base of partner organisations which GLT was instantly able to engage with. In year one GLT engaged 44 participants in this programme, working with The Albany School, a Pupil Referral Unit in Bury

Tree felling and team work

St Edmunds, and students from King Edward VI Upper School in Bury St Edmunds. Students from The Albany began attending in March 2013, initially in groups of three. These learners, who had already been excluded from mainstream schooling, were very challenging to engage in the project. The sporadic nature of attendance made development with this group difficult and no qualifications were delivered, although small gains were evident in the behaviour of individuals. In year one GLT worked with 14 year 10 students from King Edward VI, in two cohorts. All of these students had been withdrawn from optional subjects at school which had been replaced by a personal and social development qualification, and none was predicted to gain five A*- C grades at GCSE. All students developed socially as well as improving their knowledge during this course. Two students from this group were invited to attend GLT for their work experience week, further strengthening their interest and allowing them to have a credible and valid experience in a real life working environment. During this week the two students assisted in building a pole barn at the Foundry, made with timber felled and processed from Frithy Wood. This experience inspired one of the students to take up a place on a carpentry course at a local college. In her feedback Chris Swancott, First Base manager at the school, commented:

"Students are working on skills needed for the local jobs market - accredited in school through a personal and social development qualification. Students look at their strengths and

weaknesses and are being supported to enable them to look at their environment out of their life experiences.

"Students who have attended The Green Light Trust have improved their attendance and motivation at KS4 and their progression to post 16 education has widened to include Easton & Otley College and apprenticeships offered through their providers.

"Students' emotional wellbeing is being addressed through a range of woodland activities where they can develop coping strategies in a natural environment, i.e. not in a classroom."

Celebrating success

The success of this engagement and the impact on the students involved inspired GLT and the school to work with 10 of these students in year 11. The students attended 14 sessions across the year, working towards a Level 1 PECS award from ABC Awards. The intention was to give them the requisite qualifications to gain direct entry on to a level 2 vocational course at college. This was something that, based on their predicted GCSE grades, they were otherwise unlikely to achieve. Of the 10 who started the course one student missed one session and the remaining nine had 100% attendance, a stark contrast to their overall school attendance for a number of the students. Eighty per cent of the students passed the qualification and 30% of them progressed on to a course at an agricultural college. Of the remaining students all progressed into further education in a range of disciplines including music, engineering, carpentry, building and catering. Shannon was one of these students. By her own admission she was a shy girl, lacking in confidence. This was exacerbated initially by her being the only girl in the group.

Extracting timber

Over the next two years, however, Shannon blossomed, gaining skills in coppicing,

Snedding felled trees

planting, woodland design and fire-lighting, all of which contributed to her gaining her ABC level 1 environmental and conservation award in summer 2014, as well as becoming the respected 'mother hen' to the rest of the lads in the group.

In June, having completed her GCSEs, Shannon offered her services as a volunteer to help with a Woodland Minds group for teenage girls, all identified with self-esteem and/or anxiety issues.

Shannon was able to pass on the skills she had learnt with GLT, as well as mentoring the girls, sharing her experiences of how her confidence had grown as a result of her time with GLT.

Summer 2014

Cutting firewood

Shannon progressed to a four year catering course at West Suffolk College. Now a keen gym goer and healthy eating enthusiast, she started driving lessons with the aim of running her own outside catering business once she is qualified. Shannon attributes much of her new found confidence to her time at Green Light Trust.

"Thank you for a lovely two years at Green Light Trust. You have taught me so many new skills and really boosted my confidence."

In year two GLT continued work with the year 11 group, as outlined above, which was completed in May. In addition to this, work with The Albany School continued and began to become more successful, in part due to the group of students settling into the programme and attending regularly. This did not last, though, and by the end of this year it was decided that the outcomes and group sizes were not conducive to funding through the HLF project. This work did continue, however, and will be discussed in a following chapter.

Marking trees for felling

In the summer of year two a new partner organisation, Kingsfield Alternative Provision, was recruited to the programme. A first woodland ACE programme was delivered with six pupils from the school participating, each with differing reasons for not attending mainstream education. The feedback from participants and the school was very positive at the end of the course and it was decided to develop a programme which would allow those attending to gain a level 1 qualification, helping them to access further education provision. This began in year two, with four of the students from this course progressing on to the programme, and was funded directly by the school. During year two GLT also worked with year 10 and 11 students from Samuel Ward Academy, Haverhill. This was a sporadic engagement with patchy attendance, and although some of the students gained some knowledge the outcomes of this engagement did not meet expectations. It was agreed that although it may be revisited in the future work with another group would not be repeated in year three.

In year three of the project GLT worked with eight students on this programme, delivering two courses. Four year 10 students from Kingsfield attended who later progressed on to another level 1 programme. A new partner was also recruited to the project, Mildenhall College Academy. Four year 10 students from the academy attended a six week woodland ACE course culminating in June 2015. All of the students maintained a 100% attendance during their time on the course and achieved an entry level 3 PECS award. Helen McMullan, Special Educational Needs Co-ordinator, reported on the outcome:

> *"We are incredibly proud of our boys who took part in the PEC Level3. They gained a lot out of it, as it gave them the opportunity to try something different outside of the normal school curriculum."*

This programme has allowed a large number of students in school and on the periphery of education the opportunity to experience the natural heritage on offer at Frithy Wood. It has had a lasting impact on a number of those involved in the project, motivating them and allowing them to access further education provision.

Celebrating achievement

Community WildSpace Volunteers

Target participants	Total participants	Percentage of target
144	91	63%

This was one of the first programmes to be delivered as part of the project, and in year one GLT delivered three training days attended by a total of 42 participants. The events were: Practical woodland management; Exploring woodland flora; and Making Charcoal and Chips. Each session gave the participants new skills and knowledge to take back to their own community WildSpace, which could then be passed on to other volunteers. Feedback from each session was positive with participants particularly keen to try the traditional skills learnt to make whistles and pegs, etc. with a view to making craft items that could be sold to support their own community woodland.

In year two three sessions were delivered to GLT's CW volunteers and one session delivered to a wider audience. The first of the three sessions encompassed surveying and understanding the archaeology of ancient woodlands. Fifteen people attended the session where they learnt how to identify ancient woodland archaeological features such as wood banks under the expert tutelage of Angus Wainwright, Archaeologist for the National Trust. Of the 15 participants all rated the course as excellent. A group of participants from the course was later recruited to continue mapping the archaeological features of the woodland, as detailed in 'Archaeology and Landscape Survey'. In August a training event for bat surveying was led by Nick Sibbet, and results from this and further surveying can be found in 'Bats recorded'. The event was attended by 11 participants. Finally, on November 11, participants attended a training event on creating small woven items, led by Sarah Dyball.

In June 2014 GLT hosted an event in Frithy Wood which was advertised nationally to look at the impact and discuss the long term effects of Ash dieback. The event was organised by The Future Trees Trust and allowed 47 participants from all over the British Isles to visit Frithy Wood where, led by industry experts on the Ash tree, sylviculture, pests and diseases, they toured the site discussing the management of the woodland and the long term prognosis for ash as a species. This was incredibly successful with many participants commenting they would like to attend a similar session in the future.

In the final year of the project one event was delivered to eight people. This left the overall percentage of the target at 63%.

Learning new skills

Woodland HEAL

Target participants	Total participants	Percentage of target
500	431	86%

As with the other programmes Woodland HEAL got off to a slow start in year one only working with a group of year 10 science students from Stour Valley Community School. During the first half of the year 43 students attended these sessions. They were led primarily by the teacher from the school who lacked the experience or time to create engaging sessions which utilised the resources in the woodland to support the curriculum. The school decided not to continue this engagement with a new group in the new academic year. At this point it became clear that to engage with schools GLT would need to offer curriculum linked sessions that were delivered primarily by GLT staff and supported by school staff. After contacting local schools it was decided that the A-level curriculum might be easier to engage with in the woodland and sessions were

Participants being animals in a food web

planned with both Environmental Studies and Biology A-level students for the new academic year. In September five Environmental Studies students visited the woodland, discussing its management, the implications of light levels and canopy structure, whilst also taking part in some team fire lighting activities. This was then repeated with a group of 17 A-level Biology students who saw at first-hand secondary succession in action and carried out straight line transects to develop field work skills and map the changes in plant communities. The combination of active learning and additional break out activities such as fire lighting proved a real success and the school booked to return with new groups in February and May 2014.

Surveying plant communities

In order to meet the target to engage with 500 students across the lifespan of the project GLT had to take a different approach. Assessing the Key Stage Two and Three curriculum highlighted areas that could be delivered in the wood as part of HEAL sessions. GLT worked with Andrew Price, a Science specialist teacher at a middle school in the Bury

All-through Academy Trust headed up by County Upper School, to design a pilot programme. This was delivered to a total of 44 gifted and talented year 6 students from each of the three middle schools in the Trust – Howard, Horringer Court and Westley – supported by members of staff from each school, and ably assisted by two science captains from County Upper, one of whom had already attended their own Woodland HEAL day. The programme was a great success and after some minor tweaks was delivered to a further 64 students from two additional schools recruited to the programme. With further groups from County Upper attending sessions towards the end of the year, a total of 184 students attended Woodland HEAL sessions in year two. In an article published in the Bury Free Press Mrs Vicky Neale, Head Teacher at County Upper, commented:

Children cutting discs

"We congratulate the Green Light Trust on its 25th Anniversary and on the work it does in this important woodland. Our all-through science curriculum has undoubtedly been enhanced by this project and we are looking forward to the next series of days in the programmes."

In year three the changes that had been implemented during year two meant that another group of 12 students from County Upper attended early in the year and new partnerships with two primary schools allowed 170 year 5 and 6 pupils to attend the Woodland HEAL sessions. The success of this programme was further underlined by two of the schools in the programme committing to pay for the sessions beyond the span of the HLF funded project.

In summary this programme, while not reaching its target, has engaged a considerable number of school aged children and young people in Frithy Wood. The changes that were made to the programme during the project ensured that the funding was used for its intended purpose.

Conclusion

GLT engaged volunteers with a wide range of health and educational challenges, the overwhelming evidence being that all felt a positive impact from their experience. In some cases the impact was significant and had clearly been able to provide a solution unavailable or undiscovered before. What is most encouraging is that the connection with nature seemed to give people back some self-confidence and self-esteem, lost during the course of losing contact through illness or disorientation with the established educational process. We proved that this method of engagement can provide a route through recovery to work experience and back into social and economic inclusion.

A LASTING AND LIVING LEGACY

Tom Brown

From a Small Beginning

The project to bring Frithy Wood back into active management was funded over a three year period. In the context of the lifetime of a woodland this could be considered as nothing more than a blink of the eye. However, GLT and the funders involved shared the desire that this period of time, although small, should be significant. When planning the management of a woodland of this nature it is important to consider the impact of any work carried out anywhere up to 150 years in the future when recruiting or planting new trees that will grow to maturity over the next century or more. If the work undertaken as part of this project were to have anything more than a cursory impact on the woodland it would need to leave a strong legacy. Initially, therefore, thoughts focused on the impact on the woodland itself, however, it soon became evident that the legacy for the people involved with the project and for Green Light Trust itself would be equally as important.

During the project, through the work carried out by the participants, four coppice areas were worked with good regeneration seen in each. Coppicing by its very nature is cyclical and sustainable, and as such should be ongoing with no real end to the process. However, as outlined in previous chapters, a 20 year coppice rotation has been implemented, with 16 years still left to run. Although the three year project has officially come to an end, GLT is still continuing to carry out works in Frithy Wood with the groups that were engaged during the project. This will allow them to carry on with the current woodland management plan, which will be updated to reflect the lessons learnt during the project as well as the influence of Ash dieback. Although managing Frithy Wood is unlikely to ever be viable as a financially self-sufficient operation, this project's developments have helped secure its future management. As outlined already, the timber created from coppicing the woodland is now used to fuel the woodchip for the boiler at the Foundry, GLT's Headquarters. This has secured a financial incentive to continue the active management of Frithy.

Chipping wood from Frithy to fuel bio-mass boiler

Whilst there is an incentive and a desire to continue the active management of the woodland, the method used to carry it out is, on the surface, not very cost effective. The cost of working with the groups GLT engages with is higher than it would be through paying contractors to carry out the work. However, this cost does not reflect the value of the wider social and public benefits that the project delivers. This can be a difficult value to calculate and assumptions need to be made about the long term costs and benefits of supporting those involved in the project.

Legacy Planning

Consequently GLT has implemented a process of legacy planning in the second half of the project. This consisted of translating the successes seen with the groups it worked with into future funded works with these groups in the wood allowing the management to continue beyond the project. A good example is one of the Pupil Referral Units, which began with a Woodland ACE programme. This was extended to a full programme working with the school across the entire academic year. Students still attend sessions in the woodland, working towards a Level 1 qualification. This is now funded directly by the school, a situation that GLT has been able to repeat with a number of the other organisations, albeit not to the same level due to the financial constraints that they face. At the time of writing (2016), GLT is also committed to continue fundraising to work with all of the project groups and has already secured funding to deliver Woodland Minds and Woodland Rescue courses for the next calendar year.

It was hoped at the outset of the project that Frithy Wood would become an asset for the local community. The heritage trail has given local people the opportunity to explore this woodland, something that would not have occurred if it was still in private ownership.

This access will continue beyond the project as more interpretation materials are installed. The project website has also been absorbed into GLT's own website and is available and kept current for future visitors to enjoy.

Outcomes and Achievements

One of the unexpected outcomes of the project was the effect it had on Green Light Trust, celebrating its 25th anniversary during the second year of the project. This project has helped GLT to refine how it engages with its communities of interest as previously outlined. It has also given GLT the confidence to become involved with other Heritage Lottery Funded projects in East Anglia by delivering a tried and tested means of engagement with members of society who are some of the furthest from the employment market. Eleven tailor made programmes have been developed to engage with these groups. This project has enabled GLT to recruit and train staff able to work with the people it engages with in the environments it manages. As a result of having access to Frithy Wood and funding through grants to develop working relationships with partner organisations and new programs of engagement, GLT has become financially more resilient through directly funded work. One example is Green Care, a programmes where GLT accesses NHS personal health care budgets to allow participants to access the sessions it delivers over a more prolonged period of time. These impacts on GLT were reflected in a review of its own governance, and the updating of its articles of association. These developments have all progressed despite the pressures on charities in the sector at a time of austerity.

As a result of the successful engagement with the broad range of communities involved with 'Restoring the Repertoire' a development strategy was formulated during the final year, which addressed both the long term development of Frithy Wood and the expansion of this method of engagement to a wider geographical audience. Initially it was felt that the project could be replicated in a number of ancient woodlands across Suffolk. As is widely reported, these woodlands are often undermanaged due to the same pressures that had led to Frithy falling into unfavourable conditions. However, further research and liaison with stake holders in the region highlighted the fact that although such woodlands existed in the region they were not necessarily geographically close to GLT's communities of interest, and the current owners could prove difficult to motivate to sell or lease them. Following discussions with Gary Battell, Suffolk County Council's Woodland Advisor, and Nick Collinson, Head of Natural & Historic Environment at Suffolk County Council, an approach was formulated whereby GLT would work with its target groups but without taking on legal ownership of the land. Long term leases or management agreements would be used to ensure GLT would be able to raise the required funds to work in the woodlands with the groups.

For GLT, one of the revelations of the 'Restoring the Repertoire' project was that while the impact on the health of the woodland was significant, for a number of participants it had

Participant Journey

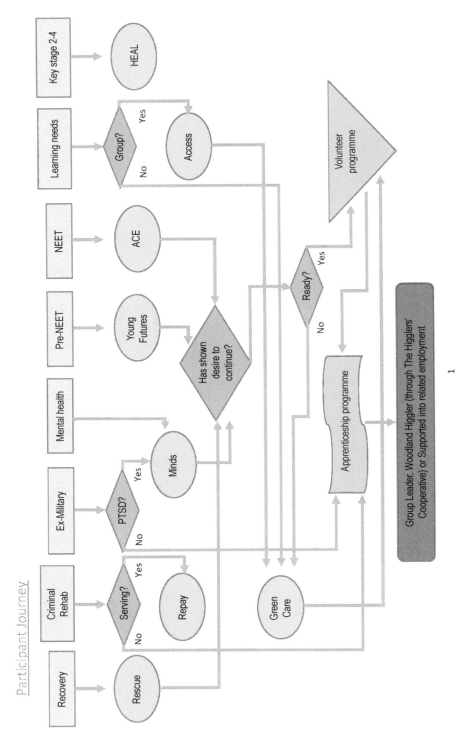

the potential to be life changing. For those individuals who clearly developed significantly as a result of the courses they attended, there needed to be route of progression so that this impact could continue. Experience indicated that roughly ten per cent of the participants on each programme showed a real aptitude and desire to progress, so it was decided that routes should be established to allow these individuals to continue developing and recovering in a supported environment.

Figure 1 shows the progression routes that were developed for participants on future programmes. The desired legacy of the project is to enable participants to progress into a volunteer role, leading to an apprenticeship and then into employment, with GLT or as a self-employed small woodland worker, historically called a Higgler. This would facilitate the establishment of a network of woodlands managed along GLT principles and perhaps also overseen by GLT. Such an approach would create economies of scale and enable capital investments in equipment to be used more widely.

Looking Forward

At the time of writing GLT is working to bring this strategy to fruition.

It is committed to raising the funds to continue the work already established in Frithy Wood, which will now begin to produce more coppice products, facilitating further training and the learning of traditional woodland skills. A second site on the outskirts of Ipswich has been leased to GLT by Suffolk County Council and work at this site, with new participants from the surrounding area, began at the end of April 2016. GLT is also using the relationships developed on another project with the RSPB at Minsmere on the Suffolk Coast, to utilise the skills learnt and is engaging groups from the Lowestoft and North Suffolk areas with funding already secured.

In conclusion GLT has considered the long term legacy of the project and work in Frithy Wood is continuing beyond the three years for which funding was originally provided. In addition, the lessons learnt from the project have been used to manage and improve the natural heritage at other locations. People involved with the project have been inspired to go on to pursue training in land based industries and many others have used the opportunity to support their own recovery from social, health, mental health or educational problems.

REFERENCES/BIBLIOGRAPHY

Foreword

Rackham, Oliver (1990). Hayley Wood: Its History and Ecology. Cambridgeshire Wildlife Trust. Cambridge.

Chapter 1

Trees of Paradise by Richard Edmunds and Nigel Hughes, Green Press. Published 1991. Forest School for all edited by Sara Knight, Sage Publications. Published 2011.

Chapter 2

A: LPFD vol.20§496(2)
B: ESRO:HA93/722/221
C: ESRO:HA93/722/220

(1) SRO (Ipswich) HB8/1/427 Book of Lawshall Rentals 1567, p. 54
(2) http://www.sssi.naturalengland.org.uk/citation/citation_photo/1001098.pdf. Status: Site of Special Scientific Interest (SSSI) notified under Section 28 of the Wildlife and Countryside Act 1981 Local Planning Authority: Babergh District Council
(3) Rackham, Oliver (1986). *The History of the Countryside*: J.M. Dent & Sons Ltd. London
(4) Rackham, Oliver (2001). *Trees and Woodland in the British Landscape*. Phoenix Press. London.
(5) ESRO: HA93 about fifty separate documents, some referred to below. It is believed that these are now held in the Ipswich SRO
(6) Hedgerow Survey 2010-2011 by Clarke & Walters to be published at a date to be confirmed by Suffolk County Council

(7) 1539/40 as in *A History of the County of Huntingdon*: Volume 2 Author: William Page, Granville Proby, S. Inskip Ladds (editors) Year published: 1932, pp. 246-250 https://www.google.co.uk/?gws_rd=ssl#q=4th+March+1539%2F40++why+two+year+dates

(8) List of Incumbents & Patrons in All Saints' Church, Lawshall

(9) **Copinger, Walter Arthur, 1847-1910** Volume: 1 *The Manors of Suffolk*. Pub: Unwin. Available online http://www.archive.org/details/manorsofsuffolkn01copiuoft

(10) A Survey of Suffolk Parish History West Suffolk Lawshall SCC researched by Wendy Goult B.A. including references from H.W.Saunders 'A bailiff's roll of the Manor of Lawshall, 1393-4'

(11) SRO (Ipswich) HA93/12/44 Survey of the Manor of Lawshall belonging to the Right Worshipful Sir Henry Lee Kt. Also the Manor of Hanningfield belonging to Sir Henry Lee. Lately purchased of Sir Robert Drury Kt.20 perches to 1in. Ralph Treswell (cartographer) 1611

(12) SRO (Ipswich) HA/93/2/483 Article of agreement

(13) SRO (Ipswich) HA93/12/45 1752 Survey of the estate at Lawshall belonging to Baptist Lee, by Thomas Warren

(14) SRO (Bury St Edmunds) HD 1180/51 *(Sep 1917)* Sale particulars Lawshall Hall Estate, Lawshall (Illus., plan)

(15) SRO Ipswich SA de Saumarez Family Archive, placed in 1960 these archives were held at Shrubland Hall but have not yet been merged into SRO HA93 catalogue

(16) Documents held by permission of Waspe family by Lawshall Archives Group

SRO: Suffolk Record Office, Gatacre Road, Ipswich, Suffolk, IP1 2LQ or 77 Raingate Street, Bury St Edmunds, IP33 2AR

ESRO: East Suffolk Record Office

PRO: Public Record Office

LPFD: (Letters and Papers Foreign and Domestic)

Chapter 3

References

(1) Oliver Rackham- 1982 survey of Frithy Wood – courtesy of Gary Battell. This document is stored in the Lawshall Archive contact elizlawshall@btinternet.com

(2) & (3) Data produced by the Wokingham District Veteran Tree Association www.wdvta.org.uk

General - Oliver Rackham - History of the Countryside - Dent - ISBN 0-460-04449-4

Oliver Rackham - The Ash Tree - Little Toller - ISBN978-1-908213-14-3

Oliver Rackham – Woodlands - Collins - ISBN 0-00-720244

Chapter 4

References

(1) **Oliver Rackham -** 1982 survey of Frithy Wood – courtesy of Gary Battell. This document is stored in the Lawshall Archive contact elizlawshall@btinternet.com

Chapter 5

References

In compiling this chapter the author consulted the following works of reference:
Lavenham Natural History Group Records 2013
The Flora of Suffolk, by Martin Sanford and Richard Fisk
Reader's Digest Field Guide to the Wild Flowers of Britain

Chapter 6

(1) Lawshall Archive Group contact elizlawshall@btinternet.com
(2) The Big Butterfly Count is a national survey of butterflies organised annually by Butterfly Conservation and carried out by members of the public. For more information and 2015 results see www.bigbutterflycount.org/about

Chapter 8

References

(1) 1981 survey of Frithy Wood, Kerridge & Clarke (unpublished)
(2) Robinson, R.A., Marchant, J.H., Leech, D.I., Massimino, D., Sullivan, M.J.P., Eglington, S.M., Barimore, C., Dadam, D., Downie, I.S., Hammond, M.J., Harris, S.J., Noble, D.G., Walker, R.H & Baillie, S.R. (2015) *BirdTrends 2015: trends in numbers, breeding success and survival for UK breeding birds. Research Report 678.* BTO, Thetford. www.bto.org/birdtrends
(3) Hayhow, D.B., Bond, A.L., Eaton, M.A., Grice, P.V., Hall, C., Hall, J., Harris, S.J., Hearn, R.D., Holt, C.A., Noble, D.G., Stroud, D.A. and Wotton, S. (2015) **The state of the UK's birds 2015**. RSPB, BTO, WWT, JNCC, NE, NIEA, NRW and SNH, Sandy, Bedfordshire

Lightning Source UK Ltd.
Milton Keynes UK
UKHW050228271118
333012UK00003B/79/P